USBORNE
BIOLOGY
FOR BEGINNERS

Lizzie Cope and
Minna Lacey

Illustrated by
Anton Hallmann
and Hannah Li

Designed by Samuel Gorham

Biology expert: Dr. Colin Dodd

CONTENTS

WHAT IS BIOLOGY?	4
LIFE AND DEATH	6
THE MEANING OF *LIFE*	8

CHAPTER 1: LIFE ON EARTH — 11
What different forms does life take, and can we make sense of the sheer variety of it all? How did life begin in the first place?

CHAPTER 2: CELLS AND DNA — 27
Find out all about cells – the tiny building blocks that are part of EVERY living thing. What is DNA, the chemical at the heart of cells?

CHAPTER 3: EVOLUTION — 47
Evolution is all about how living things change, very gradually. How does it work? Why do some creatures survive, while others die out? And how did anyone manage to hit upon and test out this grand idea?

CHAPTER 4: THE HUMAN BODY — 59
There's one kind of living thing that biologists are more interested in than any other. It's us – human beings. What are we made of? How do our bodies work? And what's so special about our brains?

CHAPTER 5: ECOLOGY — 71
Ecology is the part of biology that studies how living things grow and change together as a group. This can mean studying small, local habitats, or it can mean looking at how life all over the world is affected by changes, such as deforestation or warming oceans.

CHAPTER 6: MICROORGANISMS 87

The very smallest living things – known as microorganisms – are some of the most fascinating. Find out about the bacteria and fungi that play a role in the cycle of life and death, help plants talk to each other, and make all sorts of things from food to medicine.

CHAPTER 7: DISEASE 95

All living things can get sick. Often, the cause is another living thing. Find out where diseases come from, how they spread, how they actually make you sick, and how to stop them.

CHAPTER 8: BIG QUESTIONS 107

There are endless questions about life that people want answers to. Some of the answers depend on clever experiments and in-depth research. Others come only from debate. For example, if it was possible to live forever, would you even want to?

BIOLOGY ALL AROUND 122
JOBS IN BIOLOGY 124
GLOSSARY 125
INDEX 126
ACKNOWLEDGEMENTS 128

USBORNE QUICKLINKS

For links to websites where you can watch exciting videos about living things, find out what biologists do and challenge yourself with quizzes, go to **usborne.com/Quicklinks** and type in the title of this book.

Usborne Publishing is not responsible for the content of external websites. Children should be supervised online. Please follow the online safety guidelines at Usborne Quicklinks.

WHAT IS BIOLOGY?

"It's about life – how it begins and how it ends."

"It's about plants and animals – like me."

"It's about a changing world and how even the tiniest living things react to those changes."

Biology is about living things – from the biggest blue whale to the tiniest bacterium or fungus – how they form, grow and behave in their surroundings. Biology is done by scientists. And, like all sciences, it's about asking questions and hunting for answers.

"I want to find out how to stop new deadly diseases from emerging and spreading around the world."

"I'm wondering, is it possible to create new life forms that don't yet exist in nature?"

"I'm fascinated by birds. I want to know how migrating birds find their way across oceans and continents to the same nesting places each year."

ZOOMING IN

Biologists like zooming in on things. That often starts with taking a closer look at a particular **organism**, or life form.

"Mmm. What are you looking at?"

"It's a dragonfly. Using a magnifying glass, I can count 10 segments on its body and examine the veins on each of its four wings."

Zooming in helps biologists find out about the basic structure of living things. To get a closer look, they use microscopes with powerful magnifying lenses. This is a job mostly done in a lab.

"What are you doing?"

"I'm looking at a dragonfly through a microscope. I'm especially interested in its huge eyes that cover most of its head."

"Using a mega powerful tool called an electron microscope, I can see thousands of hexagonal – six-sided – lenses and tiny hairs on each eye. WOW!"

"If I zoomed in even closer, I could see things called CELLS. These are the building blocks that make up all living things."

LIFE AND DEATH...

...and everything in between: that's what biology is all about. It covers a huge range of topics, many of them related. Within each topic, scientists ask all kinds of questions.

Can you stop animals from becoming extinct?

How do wood frogs survive being frozen in winter?

Are all bodies the same on the inside?

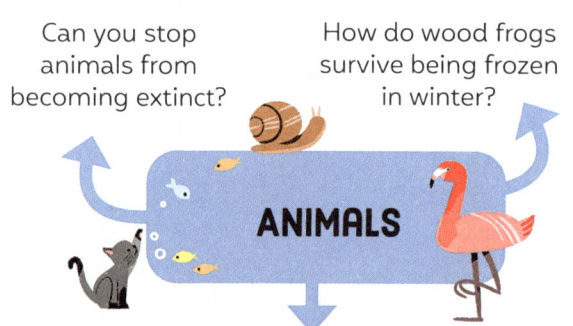

ANIMALS

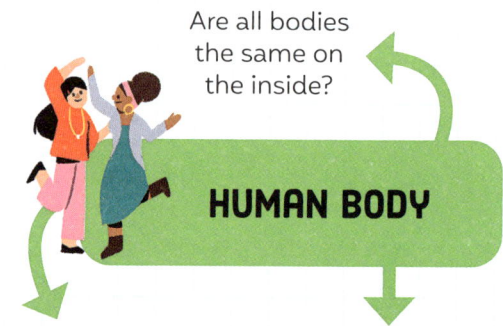

HUMAN BODY

People who study animals are known as **zoologists**, **veterinary scientists** and **marine biologists**.

How can exercise help heal broken bones?

This is the work of **anatomists** and **physiologists**.

How old is the oldest tree?

Is algae good for the planet?

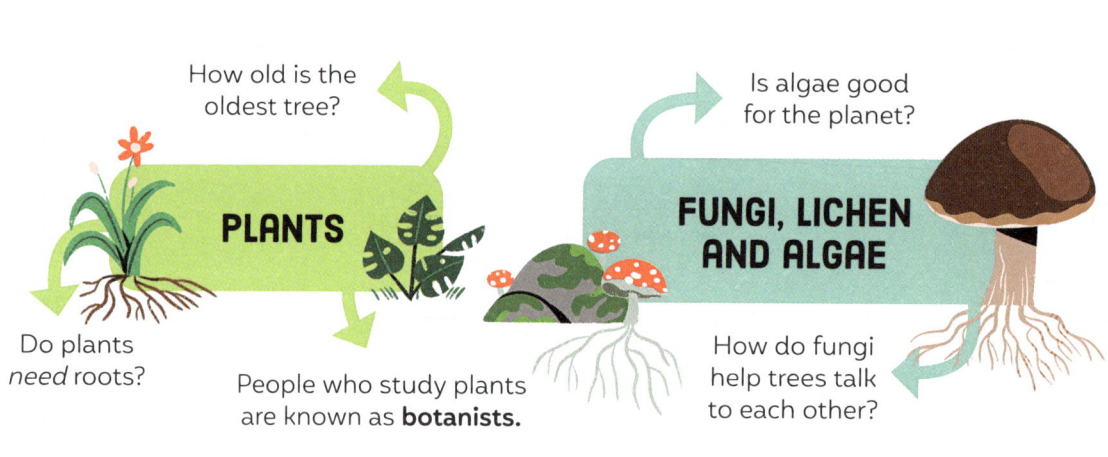

PLANTS

FUNGI, LICHEN AND ALGAE

Do plants *need* roots?

People who study plants are known as **botanists.**

How do fungi help trees talk to each other?

When did life begin?

Are humans still gradually changing, or evolving?

Wow! I never knew biology covered so many things.

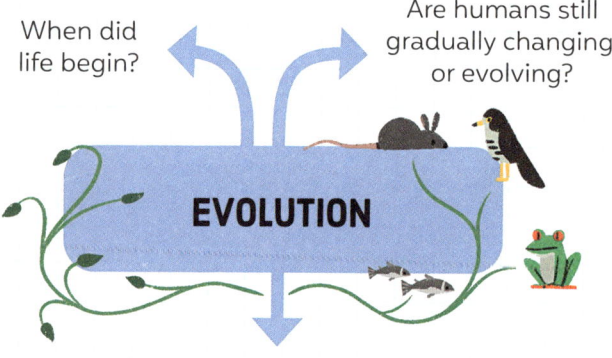

EVOLUTION

Is there anything that all plants and animals have in common?

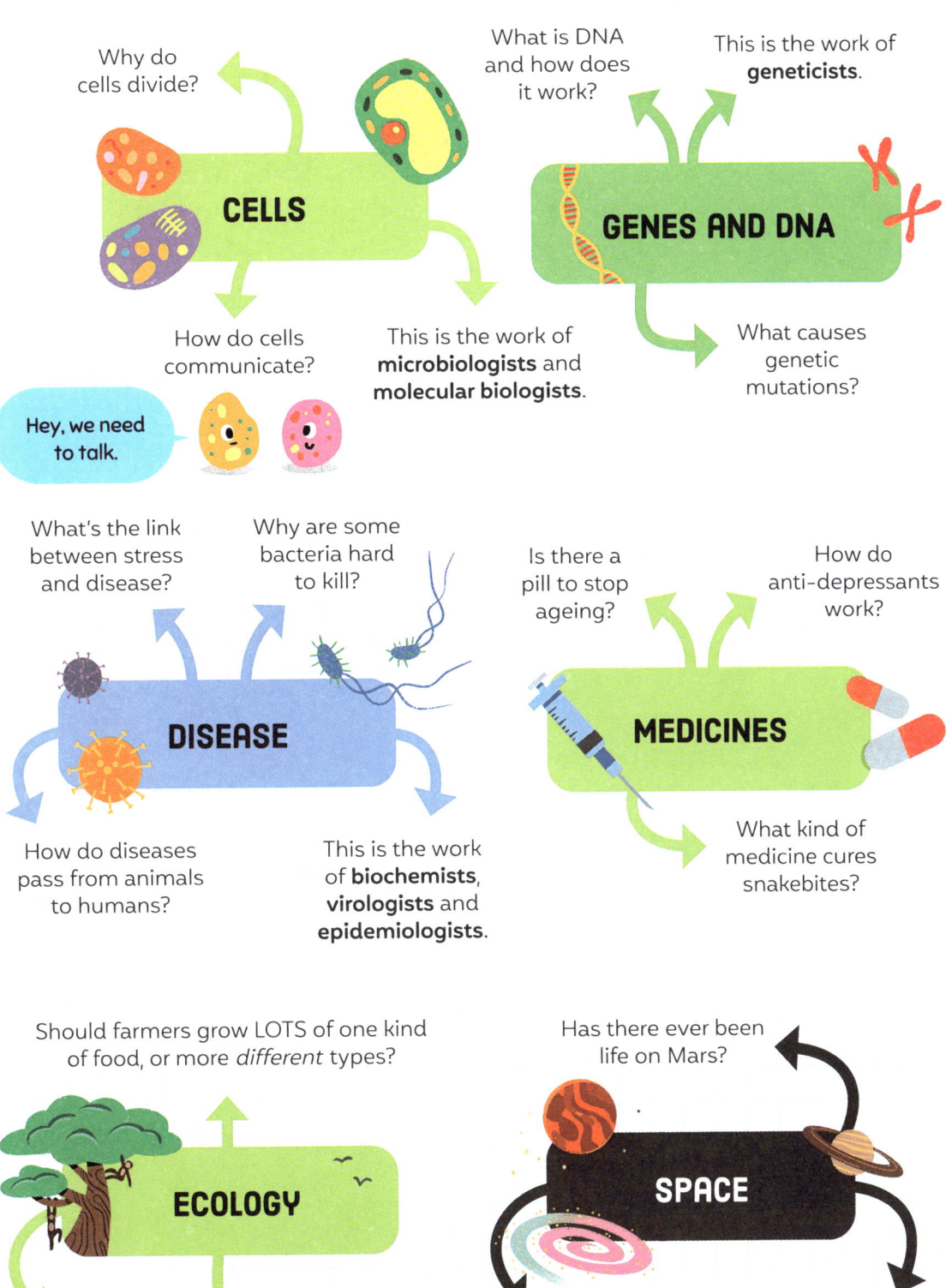

THE MEANING OF *LIFE*

Each individual living thing is called an **organism**. Every organism, big or small, has seven main things in common. Most biologists agree that for something to be defined as "living", it has to...

...CONSUME FOOD
Organisms get the energy they need by eating, or taking in nutrients.

Most plants use sunlight to make their own food through a process called **photosynthesis**.

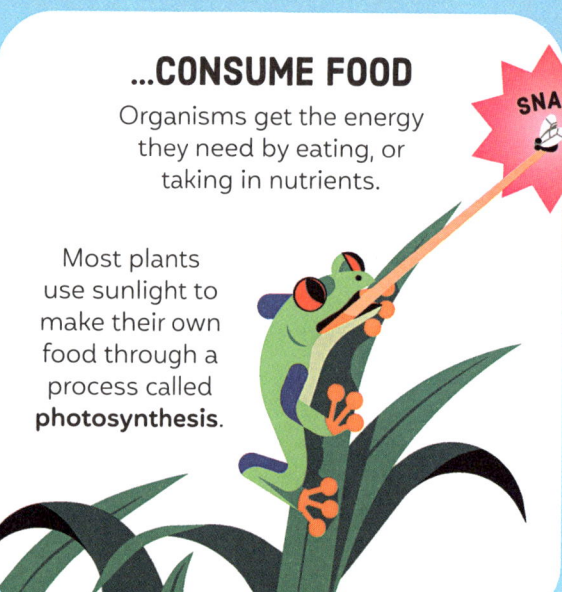

SNAP!

...USE ENERGY
Everything an organism does uses energy, whether it's moving, growing, or simply staying still.

...EXCRETE
All organisms produce waste, such as dung, urine, sweat or gases.

BUUURP

ARRRGH

...GROW
Most organisms get bigger by adding new cells.

I'm a single-celled organism. I just get larger.

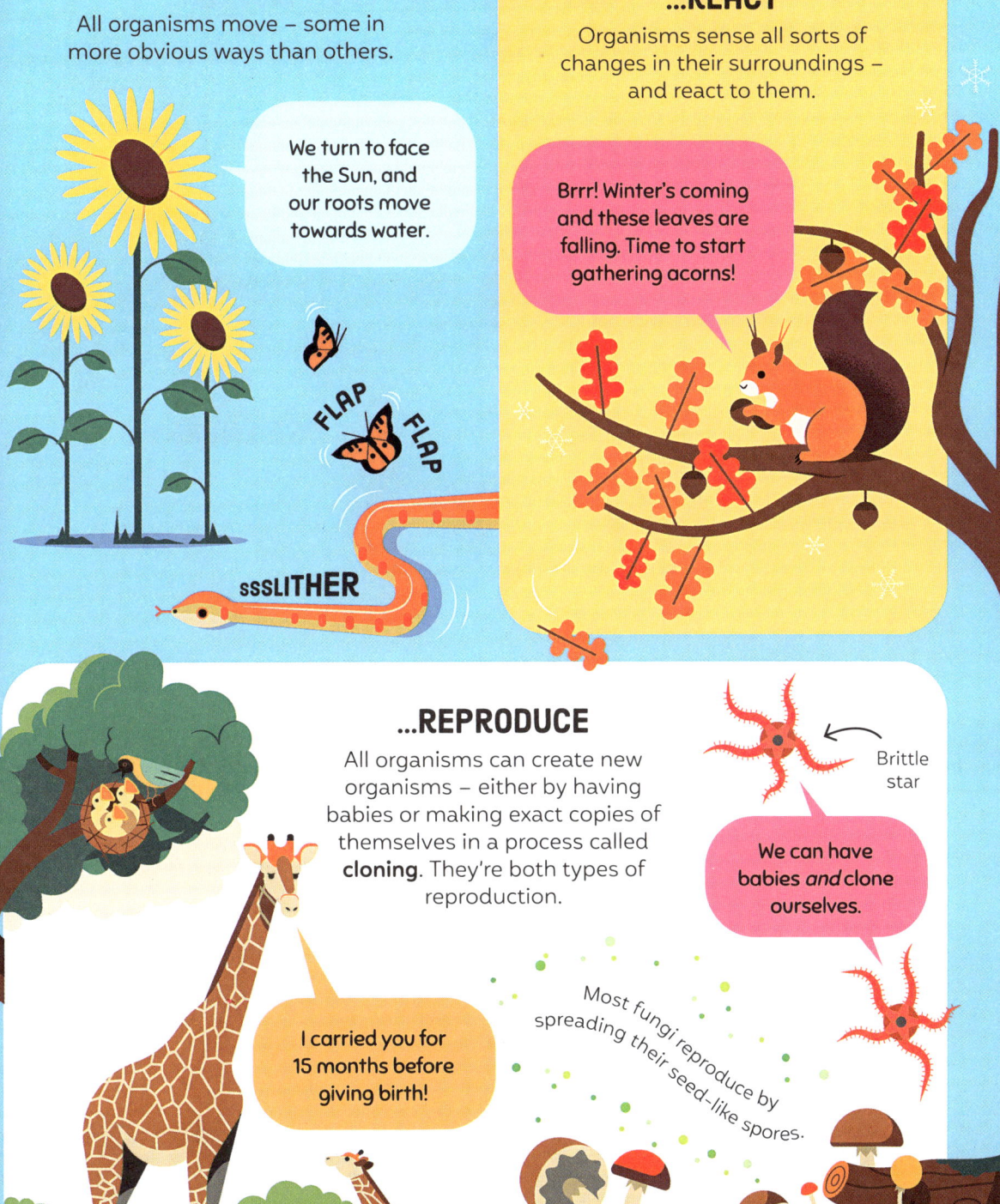

CHAPTER 1
LIFE ON EARTH

As far as we know, Earth is a planet like no other. That's because it has LIFE – in fact it's teeming with trillions of living things of all shapes and sizes.
Why it does is one of the greatest mysteries in the universe.

Where did life begin? What did the earliest life forms look like and how did they develop into the huge variety of living things on our planet today?

We may never know exactly what happened. But a large part of biology involves detective work. Scientists gather evidence, piece it together and form different theories.

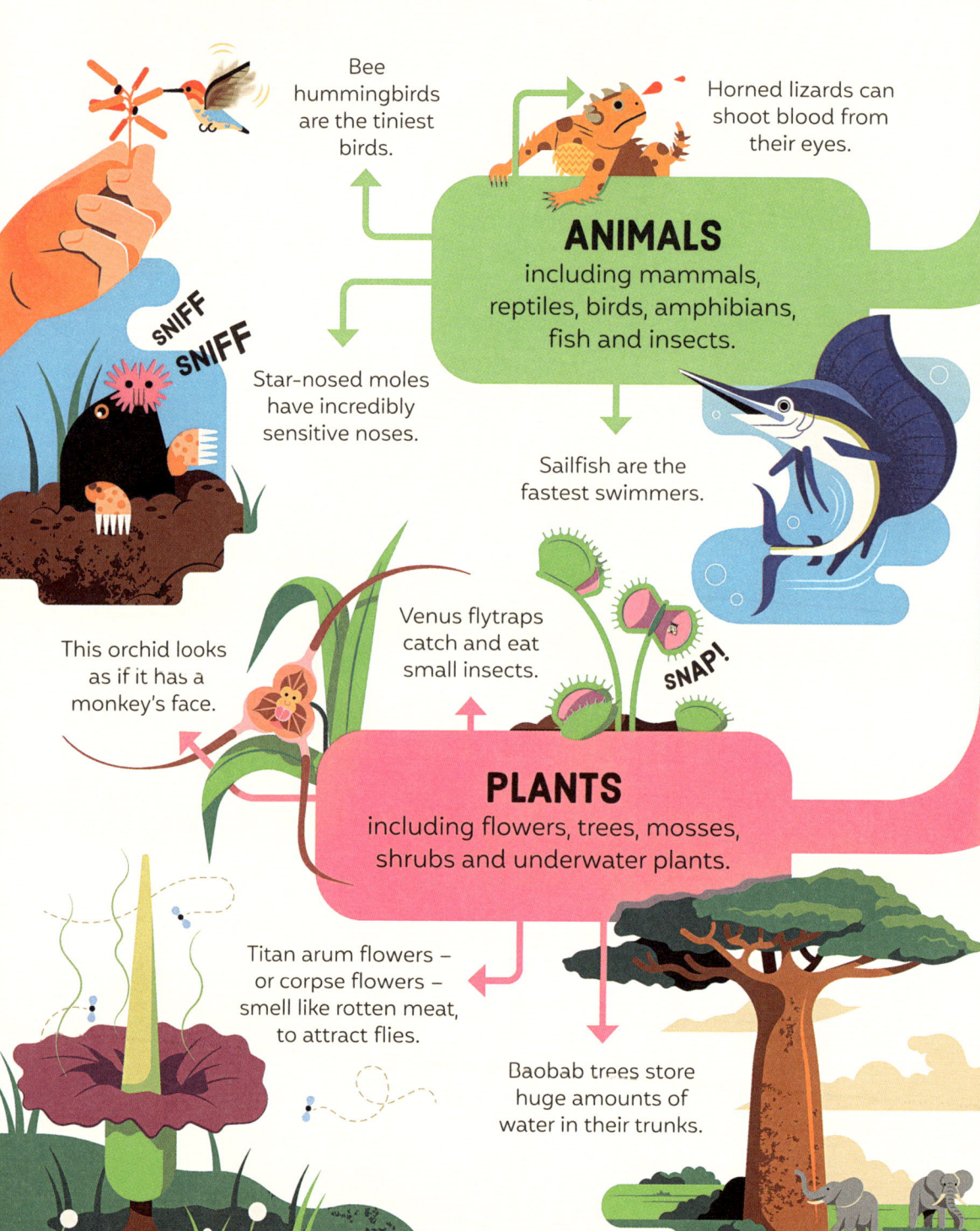

Death cap mushrooms get their name because they're deadly poisonous.

They're poisonous to humans, but not to me! Weaklings.

FUNGI

including mushrooms, mould and yeast. (*Fungi* is the plural of fungus.)

Jack O'Lantern mushrooms glow in the dark.

Penicillin is a type of mould that can be used as medicine.

PROTISTS

are neither animals, plants nor fungi. Many are plant-like organisms that live in damp or underwater places.

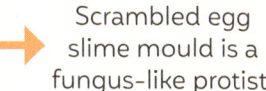

Scrambled egg slime mould is a fungus-like protist.

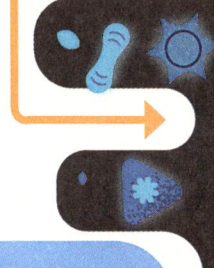

All types of algae are protists – and giant kelp is the largest.

Diatoms are tiny, sea-dwelling algae. They produce 30% of the world's oxygen.

PROKARYOTES

are single-celled organisms that come in two main types: bacteria and archaea.

Bacteria   Archaea

We may look like bacteria, but scientists often put us in a category of our own. Find out more on page 35.

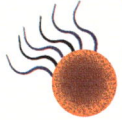 

Bacteria and archaea are microscopically tiny. They live all over the planet – on land, in the sea and even in your body.

WHAT'S YOUR CLASSIFICATION?

To help make sense of living things, biologists group them into further categories called **ranks**. This process is known as **classification** and the entire grouping system is called **taxonomy**. It's based on how different types of organisms are related.

GIRAFFE TAXONOMY

KINGDOM:
Animalia
(all animals)

PHYLUM:
Chordata
(has a backbone)

Also includes:
- Birds
- Fish
- Reptiles

CLASS:
Mammalia
(has warm blood and produces milk for its young)

Also includes:
- Humans
- Dogs
- Horses

What's MY classification? I know I'm in the animal kingdom...

You are. Within that, the next rank is a PHYLUM. You're in the same phylum as me and every other animal with a backbone.

So we're related?

Very distantly. Within our phylum we humans and you giraffes are also in the same CLASS – mammals.

Looks like that's where our similarities end.

ORDER:
Artiodactyla
(has even-toed hooves)

Also includes:
- Cows
- Camels
- Reindeer

FAMILY:
Giraffidae
(has horn-like bumps on head)

Also includes:
- Okapi

GENUS:
Giraffa

Includes:
- All giraffes

SPECIES:
Northern giraffe, also known as:
Giraffa camelopardalis

Each species has a two-part scientific name in Latin. It's usually written in italics.

Correct. The next rank is ORDER. Every mammal in yours has similar hooves.

But very different shoe sizes.

In the next rank – your FAMILY – you only have one relative. It's the okapi.

I don't see much resemblance.

Maybe not. But giraffes and okapi actually share around 98% of their DNA*.

Wow!

Finally, here's your GENUS – giraffe – and your exact SPECIES... you're a Northern giraffe!

*Find out about DNA on page 22.

WHOSE IDEA WAS IT?

The system of taxonomy was first developed in the 18th century by a Swedish biologist named Carl Linnaeus. His aim was simple – but perhaps impossible to achieve – to name, describe and organize *every type of living thing on Earth.*

I shall group organisms together based on their physical features!

These butterflies all have similar-shaped wings. I'll classify them in the same genus, which I'll call *Papilio*.

Papilio demoleus

Papilio machaon

Papilio nireus

Linnaeus was the first to develop a two-part naming system called **binomial nomenclature**.

Papilio podalirius

Papilio glaucus

The first part tells you the genus.

The second part tells you the exact species.

Since Linnaeus's time, millions of species have been classified and named using the taxonomic system. It's incredibly useful. It provides a clear structure that scientists all around the world can use to catalogue living things, and identify new ones.

Today, biologists no longer classify organisms based on their appearance. Instead, they can tell how closely different species are related by comparing their DNA. You can find out more about DNA on page 22.

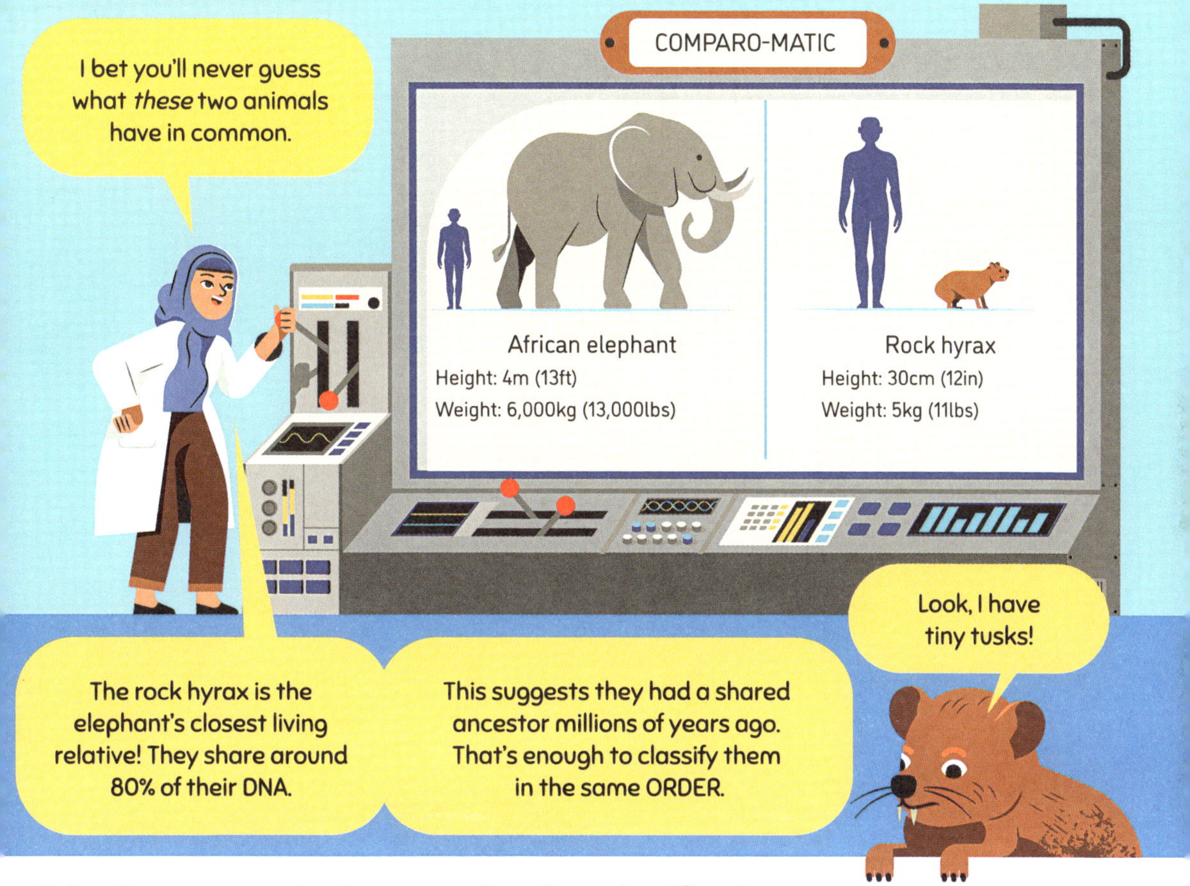

COMPARO-MATIC

African elephant
Height: 4m (13ft)
Weight: 6,000kg (13,000lbs)

Rock hyrax
Height: 30cm (12in)
Weight: 5kg (11lbs)

"I bet you'll never guess what *these* two animals have in common."

"Look, I have tiny tusks!"

"The rock hyrax is the elephant's closest living relative! They share around 80% of their DNA."

"This suggests they had a shared ancestor millions of years ago. That's enough to classify them in the same ORDER."

Scientists constantly change and update classifications as new evidence comes to light.

"These birds of prey look so similar, we once thought they MUST be closely related."

"Wrong! Their DNA reveals that a falcon is more similar to a parakeet than a hawk."

Cooper's hawk

Peregrine falcon

Parakeet

"I'm far more fabulous, though."

HOW DID LIFE BEGIN?

No one knows for sure how life on Earth started, or even what it looked like – it's a huge mystery. But scientists have come up with all sorts of theories.

THEORY 1: PRIMORDIAL SOUP + LIGHTNING

In the 1900s, a popular theory was that life began from a mix of chemicals in Earth's early oceans, known as **primordial soup**. In 1952, American scientists Stanley Miller and Harold Urey tested this theory with an experiment.

This groundbreaking experiment showed that life *could* have developed naturally from a combination of chemicals. But it didn't *prove* the theory. Even if amino acids did form in this way, there's no guarantee that they assembled into something that was alive.

THEORY 2: ALIEN MICROORGANISMS

Some scientists believe that life didn't begin on Earth at all, but that living microorganisms are scattered through the universe, carried by space dust.

This could mean that microorganisms came to Earth on a crash-landing comet or meteor.

We know some microorganisms CAN survive in space because astronauts have taken them up there from Earth.

But we've never found any evidence that they live there already...

THEORY 3: DEEP OCEAN VENTS

One of the most popular theories today is that life began in chimney-like structures called **hydrothermal vents**, deep down on the ocean floor. The superheated vents churn out all the chemical ingredients needed for life.

It's difficult to recreate these extreme conditions in a lab. But scientists can simulate them on computers.

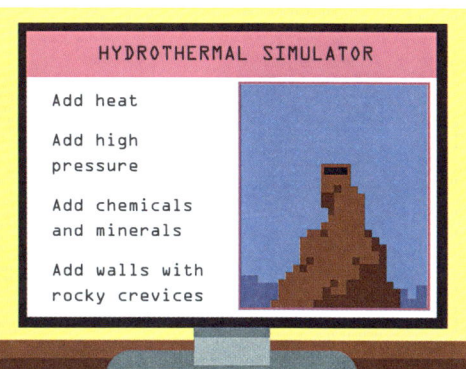

HYDROTHERMAL SIMULATOR

Add heat

Add high pressure

Add chemicals and minerals

Add walls with rocky crevices

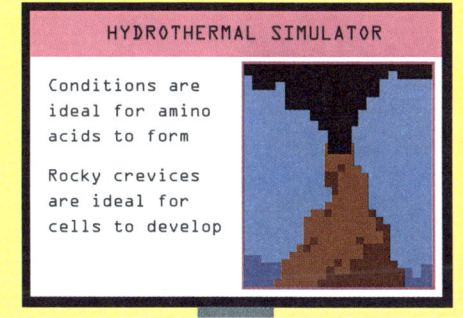

HYDROTHERMAL SIMULATOR

Conditions are ideal for amino acids to form

Rocky crevices are ideal for cells to develop

Wow!

It's possible that all three theories have some truth to them.

SEARCHING FOR EVIDENCE

We may not know exactly *how* life started, or what the very first life form was, but there's one thing scientists know for sure. Life has existed on Earth for at least 3.5 BILLION years.

Some of the oldest known organisms are tiny, plant-like organisms called **cyanobacteria**.

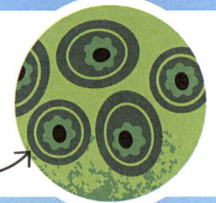

They formed large clumps on the Earth's surface. Many of them lived where Western Australia is today.

Were cyanobacteria the first living things then?

Probably not. But they're the oldest ones we know about.

But HOW do we know about them? Surely they're long gone?

They are. But we can find clues in something that's lasted much longer – rocks.

Rocks? What can they tell us?

Lots! THESE rocks contain biomarkers – chemical imprints that could only have come from living things.

Cool! What else?

Rocks can tell us what gases were in the atmosphere long ago. This helps us figure out what kinds of organisms could have survived back then. But that's not all...

CLUES TRAPPED IN TIME

Most of our knowledge about ancient life comes from **fossils** – traces of living things that were preserved in rocks long, long ago. Here's what happened...

3.5 BILLION YEARS AGO
Cyanobacteria clumped together in lumpy mounds on the Earth's surface. They produced thin layers of a rocky substance called calcium carbonate.

Cyanobacteria

As more cyanobacteria grew on each mound, they built up more and more layers of calcium carbonate.

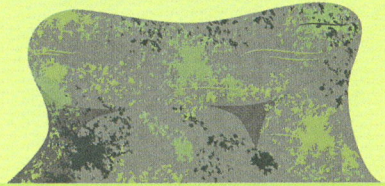

3,000 YEARS LATER
Eventually, all the cyanobacteria in each mound died, but the rocky structures remained. These are fossils.

TODAY
Scientists can identify cyanobacteria fossils from the layers of calcium carbonate. They use a process called **radiometric dating** to tell how old they are.

Rocks give off small amounts of radiation which we can measure to calculate their age.

These rocks are 3.5 billion years old. So that's when the cyanobacteria must have lived.

Case solved!

ANCIENT ANCESTOR

Many scientists believe that every living thing on Earth today is descended from a single organism known as LUCA (the Last Universal Common Ancestor).

Scientists can only guess what LUCA might have looked like, or where and when it lived – that is, if it even lived at all.

It was probably a single-celled organism.

It may well have lived in the ocean.

We think it lived around 4 billion years ago... give or take a few million years.

There's no physical evidence for LUCA – at least not in fossils. The reason scientists think it existed is because of clues in organisms that are alive *today*. These clues are in a part of each cell, called **DNA**.

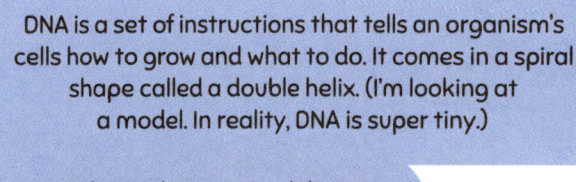

DNA is a set of instructions that tells an organism's cells how to grow and what to do. It comes in a spiral shape called a double helix. (I'm looking at a model. In reality, DNA is super tiny.)

Every living thing on Earth has DNA. And every single bit of DNA from every organism has some basic similarities.

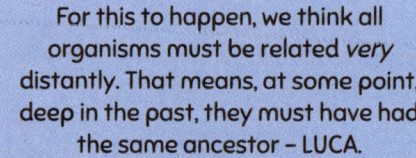

For this to happen, we think all organisms must be related *very* distantly. That means, at some point, deep in the past, they must have had the same ancestor – LUCA.

HISTORY OF LIFE ON EARTH

The development of life from simple cells to complex organisms hasn't been easy. But, even against the odds, life has always managed to survive and evolve. Here are some of the landmarks along the way.

3.5 billion years ago
Cyanobacteria first appeared – the oldest life forms to have left fossils.

2 billion years ago
More complex cells, called eukaryotes, began to develop.

445 million years ago
Earth's climate got colder and around 85% of all species died out.

4 billion years ago
Scientists think LUCA lived around this time.

1 billion years ago
Some early types of fungi may have lived in the oceans around this time.

530 million years ago
An explosion of different animals, including fish, rapidly evolved in the oceans.

4.5 billion years ago
Planet Earth formed. Later, the oceans formed too.

800 million years ago
Animals began evolving. Some of the first were sea sponges.

700 million years ago
Plants may have started to grow on land. They evolved from algae in the oceans.

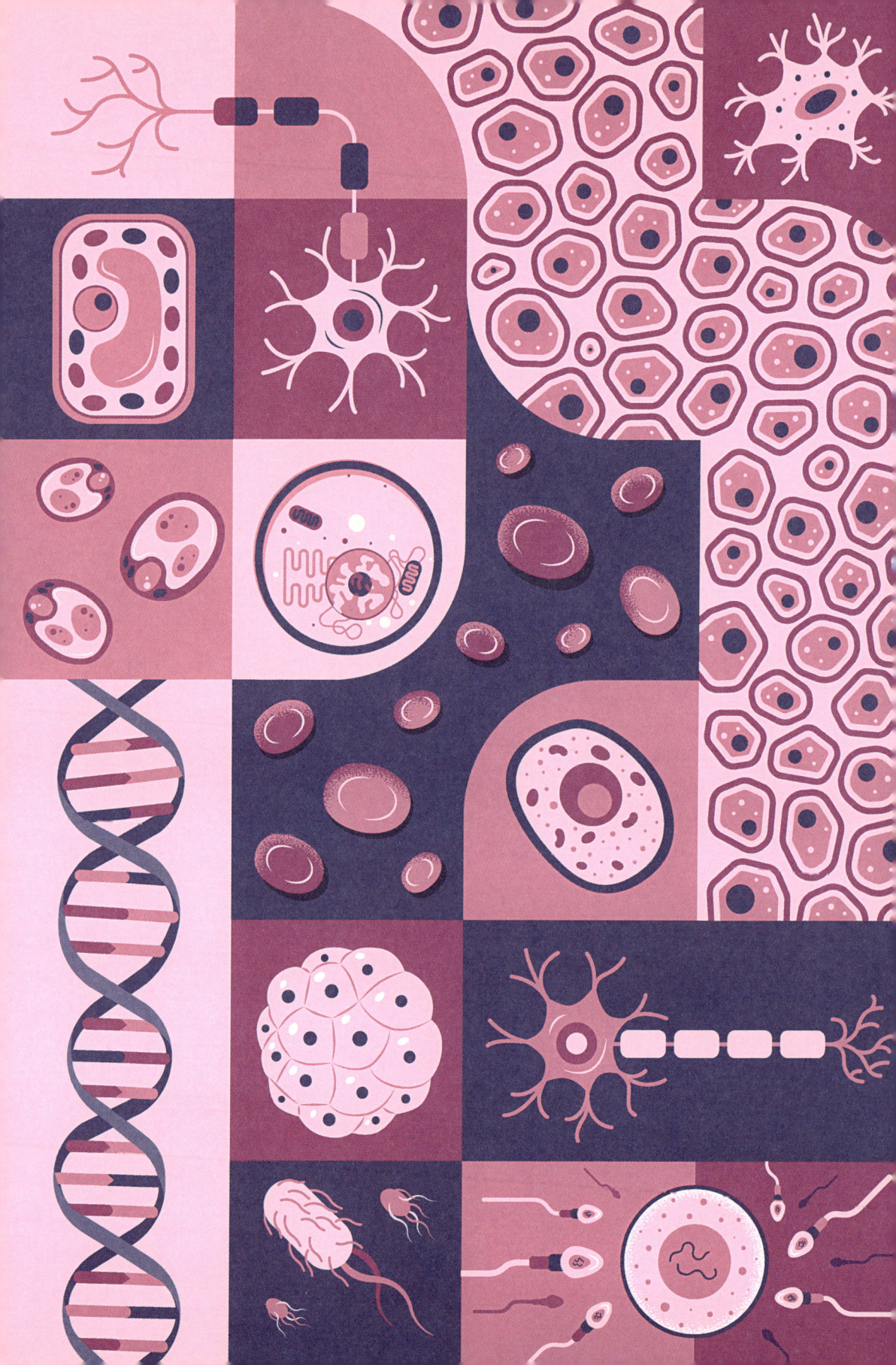

CHAPTER 2
CELLS AND DNA

Why do trees grow so tall and live so long? Why do whales have no legs? Why do some mushrooms glow in the dark? To explain this remarkable variety of life, biologists look for the answers in CELLS.

All living things begin as a single cell. Some cells copy themselves to make billions more cells, which develop into complex organisms.

One of the biggest discoveries scientists have made about cells is the DNA they carry inside them. This is one of those mysterious things that – no matter how much is revealed about it – leads to more and more questions.

WHAT ARE CELLS?

All living things are made of cells. As well as joining together to make different organisms, cells do all kinds of jobs, such as turning food into energy and helping living things to grow.

Some living things, such as bacteria (the name for more than one *bacterium*) or yeast, are made of just ONE CELL.

Bacteria

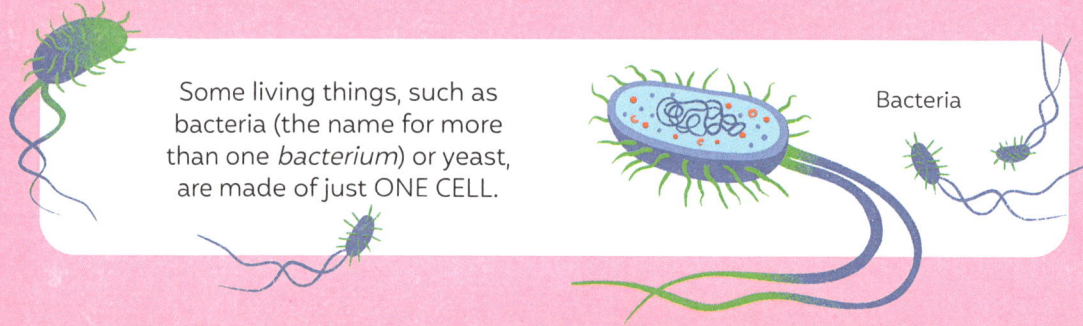

Most living things that we can see, such as animals, are made of BILLIONS of cells all clinging together. They're known as **multicellular** – which means *many cells*. In general, bigger life forms have millions more cells than smaller ones.

What about me? How many cells are there in *my* body?

An ant is made up of about 20 million cells.

Humans contain about 30 trillion cells – that's 30 million million cells.

Mmmm

This strawberry has about 1 million cells.

Cells really are VERY small. For instance, you could fit 250 human red blood cells on the head of this pin, which is 2mm (0.08in) wide.

WHAT'S INSIDE A CELL?

All cells contain various tiny parts designed to carry out different jobs. These parts are known as **organelles**. Here are some of them.

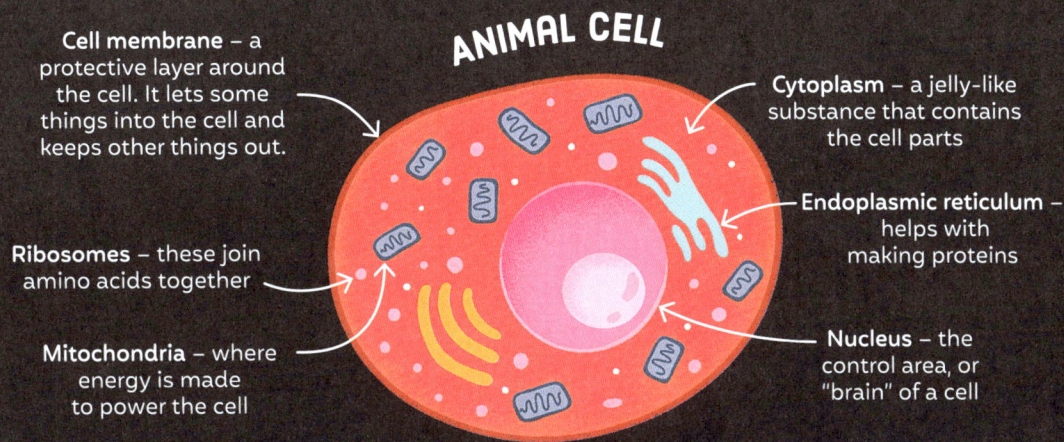

ANIMAL CELL

- **Cell membrane** – a protective layer around the cell. It lets some things into the cell and keeps other things out.
- **Cytoplasm** – a jelly-like substance that contains the cell parts
- **Endoplasmic reticulum** – helps with making proteins
- **Ribosomes** – these join amino acids together
- **Mitochondria** – where energy is made to power the cell
- **Nucleus** – the control area, or "brain" of a cell

All cells contain a set of instructions inside them called **DNA**. Precise instructions for different functions are carried in **genes** – short sections of DNA. In plants and animals, DNA is found in the nucleus.

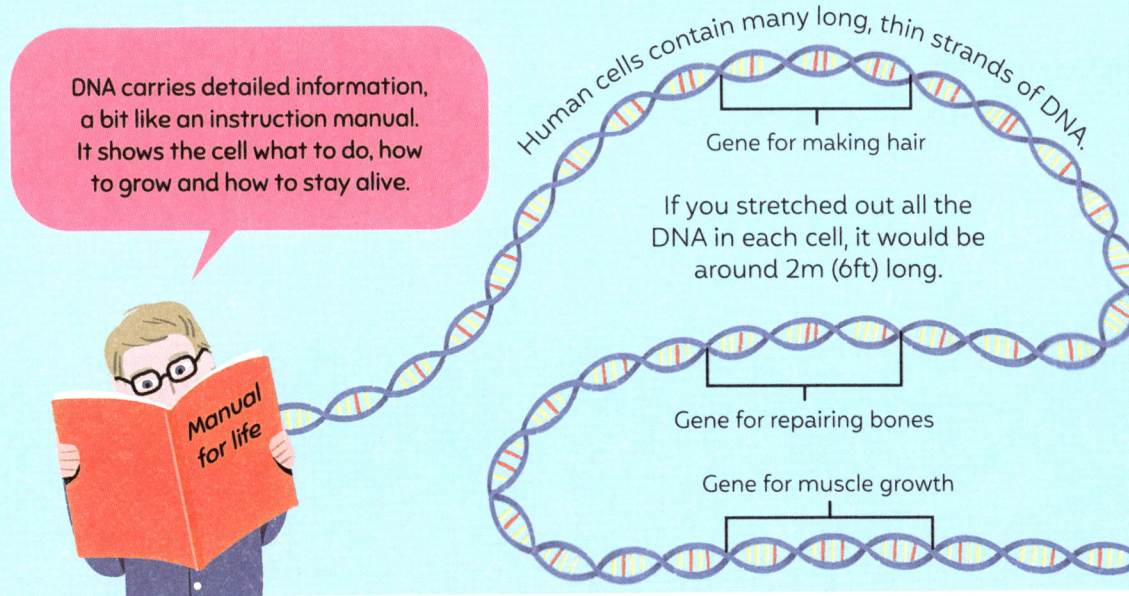

DNA carries detailed information, a bit like an instruction manual. It shows the cell what to do, how to grow and how to stay alive.

Manual for life

Human cells contain many long, thin strands of DNA.

Gene for making hair

If you stretched out all the DNA in each cell, it would be around 2m (6ft) long.

Gene for repairing bones

Gene for muscle growth

One aim in biology is to question how different life forms behave. Many of the answers can be found by examining their cells – in particular, their genes and DNA. This is a relatively new area of study for biologists.

DISCOVERING CELLS

Some discoveries depend on having the right equipment. Until around 400 years ago, nobody knew about cells. But when people began experimenting with lenses and microscopes, it became possible to *see* cells for the first time.

In the 1660s, British scientist Robert Hooke was curious about observing tiny creatures, and making drawings and notes about them.

"If only I could see that flea more closely..."

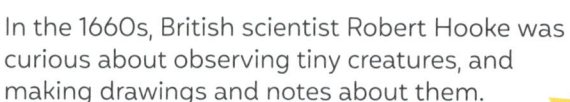

In 1665, he invented a microscope with two lenses that magnified things to 50 TIMES their original size.

One thing he examined was a tiny living louse that had bitten him. He was able to see it in incredible detail.

He observed lots of tiny holes, or chambers, inside cork, a type of tree bark. The holes resembled "cells" – the rooms where monks live in a monastery.

"I can see my blood in its belly!"

"I'll call these chambers CELLS!"

In 1665, Hooke published a book called *Micrographia*, the first book to show detailed drawings of plants and animals as seen through a microscope.

"How terrifying, a GIANT FLEA! My body is itching."

"What are these *cells* he writes about?"

"No idea."

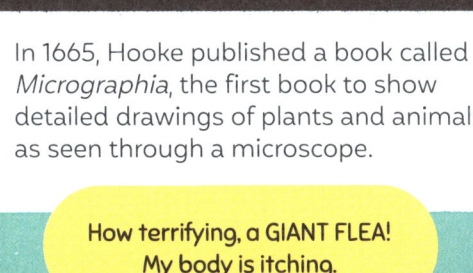

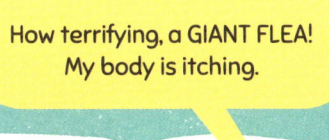

Although Hooke observed large structural cells in cork, he wasn't the first to observe and name similar parts inside animals...

In 1666, Dutch cloth merchant, Antonie van Leeuwenhoek, invented a simple one-lens microscope to look at fabric. It enlarged things by a whopping 275 TIMES.

Van Leeuwenhoek microscope

Using his microscope, van Leeuwenhoek found bacteria in rainwater. He was the first to see any sort of microorganism, although he named them "animalcules".

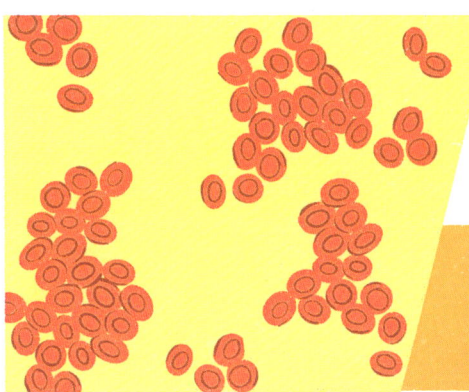

In 1673, he noted "round globules" in samples of his own blood and became the first person to identify red blood cells.

These early microscopes gave the first glimpse of what cells looked like, from the empty chambers – or cell walls – of dead plant cells, to living bacteria. The race was now on among scientists everywhere to find out everything they could about cells.

CELLS EVERYWHERE

Biologists have found cells, from all kinds of organisms, in every part of the planet – from swamps and mountaintops to the deepest cracks in the sea floor. They've identified many different types of cells *within* each organism, too.

Here are some of the different ones found in your body.

Red blood cells

Flat and wide to absorb as much oxygen as possible

Bone cells

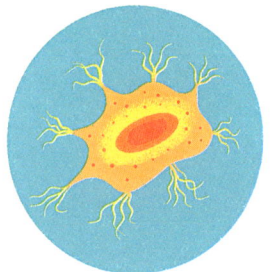

Branches at the ends let them link easily with other bone cells to help with bone repair

Fat cells

Soft and round to store energy and cushion the body

Human cells are not the only cells in your body. Over half your cells are non-human. They belong to single-celled organisms, such as bacteria, also known as **microorganisms**.

Microorganisms live in your skin, including inside your pores and around your hairs.

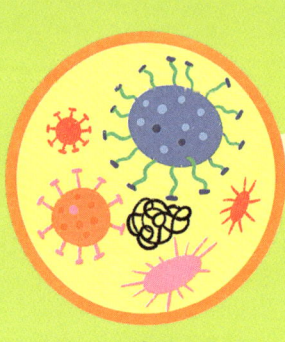

Billions of bacteria, fungi, viruses and archaea live in your nose, mouth and ears.

About 100 trillion microorganisms live in your gut.

Most non-human cells in your body are *friendly* cells that do essential things, such as help you digest food and absorb vitamins, fight infection and enable your body to run smoothly.

Finding out which types of cells survive in which places is a key part of biology. It helps answer questions about why cells and organisms develop in such different ways and where cells come from.

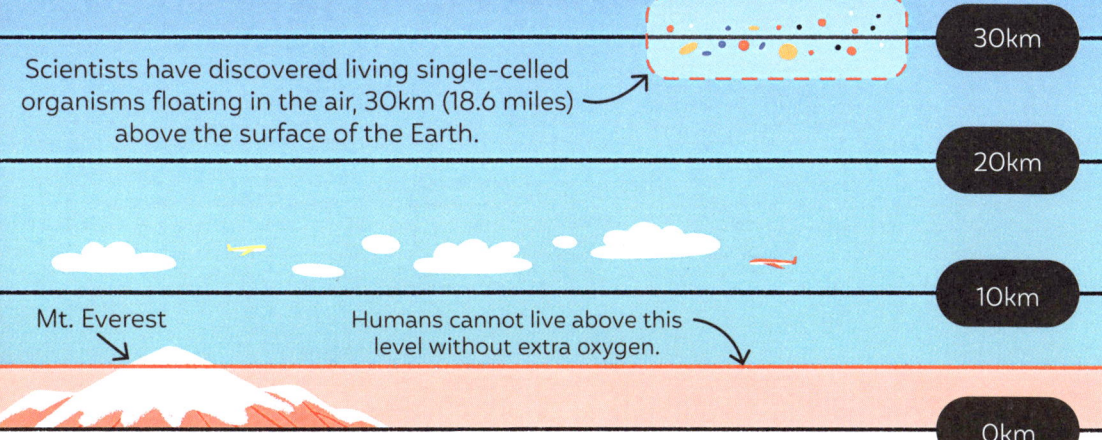

Scientists have discovered living single-celled organisms floating in the air, 30km (18.6 miles) above the surface of the Earth.

30km

20km

10km

Mt. Everest

Humans cannot live above this level without extra oxygen.

0km

ADVENTUROUS ARCHAEA

Biologists are particularly fascinated by archaea cells, because they can survive in extreme environments, where no other life forms exist.

We flourish in hot springs...

60°C (140°F)

...and hydrothermal vents, where gas and minerals burst from the ocean floor.

100°C (212°F)

We live in ice within glaciers...

−17°C (1.4°F)

...and in salty lakes, where there's little oxygen.

For all these reasons, archaea are considered to be organisms that are likely to survive a space flight and may live on other planets (see page 108).

33

CELL STRUCTURE

To understand how cells work, scientists have classified and studied the organelles inside them. Organelles carry out essential jobs that help cells – and the organisms themselves – live and grow.

Here are the organelles of a plant cell.

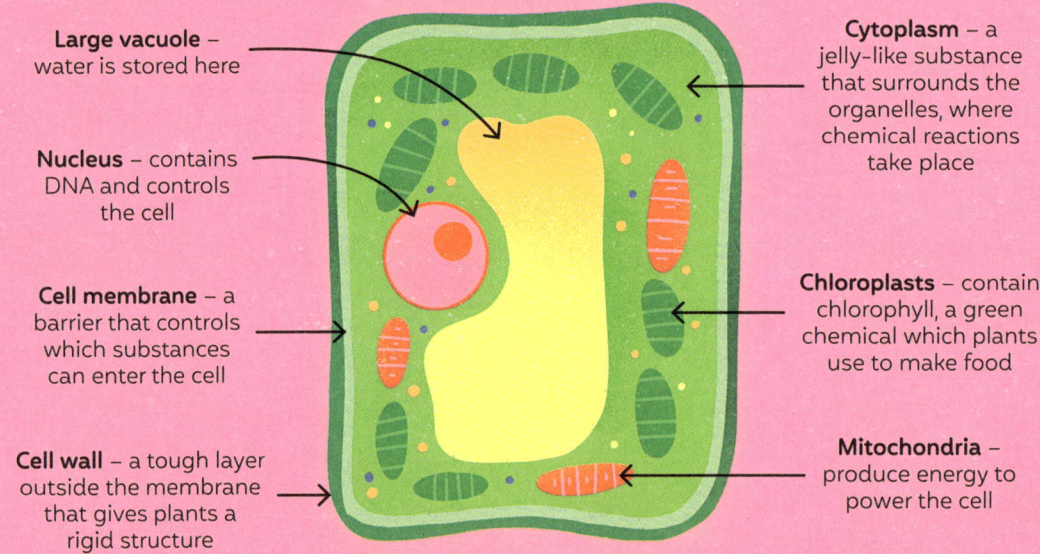

Large vacuole – water is stored here

Nucleus – contains DNA and controls the cell

Cell membrane – a barrier that controls which substances can enter the cell

Cell wall – a tough layer outside the membrane that gives plants a rigid structure

Cytoplasm – a jelly-like substance that surrounds the organelles, where chemical reactions take place

Chloroplasts – contain chlorophyll, a green chemical which plants use to make food

Mitochondria – produce energy to power the cell

Why do we need to learn all these tricky names? Can't we find out about plants just by watching them grow from the outside?

Yes, you can, and that's important too. But the insides of a cell reveal exactly how and why a plant grows the way it does.

For instance, when water enters a plant cell, it fills the large vacuole. The vacuole expands and presses against the cell wall. This makes the cell rigid and stops the plant from wilting. That's how stems that look flimsy support heavy flowers.

THREE TYPES OF LIFE

Scientists have compared the cells of thousands of different organisms, from ants and beetles to bacteria and algae. In 1990, after examining them in detail, they came up with an important discovery...

There are three main forms of life on Earth.

BACTERIA

We're single-celled organisms with no nucleus. Our DNA is coiled loosely inside us.

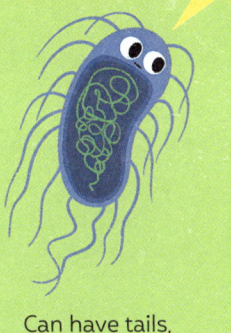

Can have tails, called **flagelli**, to help them move

Can cause diseases

Destroyed by antibiotics

ARCHAEA

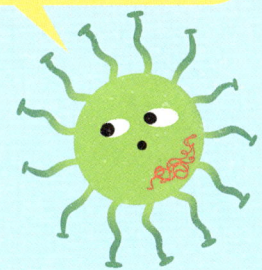

Can have flagelli

Do not cause disease

Resist antibiotics

Tough cell walls help them survive in extreme conditions

EUKARYOTES

We're multi-celled organisms. Our cell DNA is contained in a nucleus.

Nucleus

Eukaryotes include **every other** life form, including humans.

Some of their cells, such as red blood cells, start out with a nucleus but lose it later.

Archaea are more closely related to eukaryotes than bacteria, because they contain similar chemicals in their DNA. This means their cells develop in similar ways.

I'm a eukaryote and so are you. And so is this banana tree. Does that mean we're the same as a banana?

No. But it means we have similar cells to a banana, similar chemicals in our DNA and similar ways of growing and reproducing.

CELL FACTS

Cells are seriously interesting. Here are just a few things biologists have uncovered about animal cells.

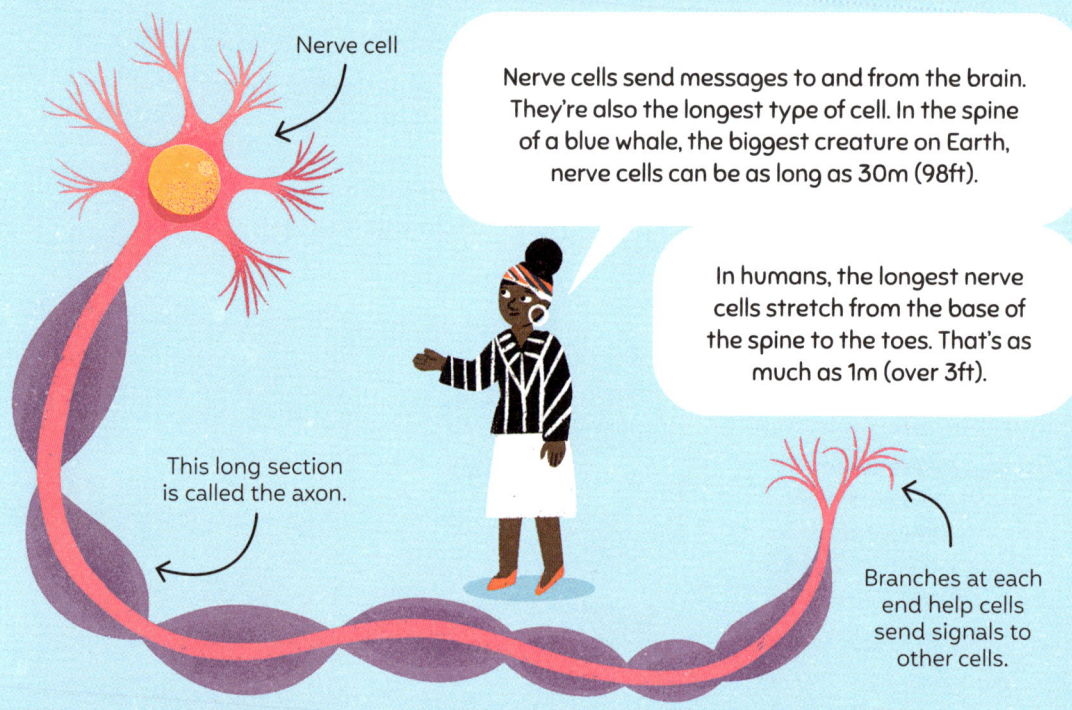

Nerve cell

Nerve cells send messages to and from the brain. They're also the longest type of cell. In the spine of a blue whale, the biggest creature on Earth, nerve cells can be as long as 30m (98ft).

In humans, the longest nerve cells stretch from the base of the spine to the toes. That's as much as 1m (over 3ft).

This long section is called the axon.

Branches at each end help cells send signals to other cells.

Cells live for different lengths of time. When they die, they are usually replaced by new ones.

Mammals, fish, amphibians and reptiles have white blood cells. Their job is to fight disease. Some white blood cells live for only a few hours.

Skin cells are replaced every 15-30 days.

Red blood cells live for 120 days.

Some eye lens cells last a lifetime.

Brain cells can live longer than the bodies they start in – if implanted into another organism. Human brain cells could live for 200 YEARS!

Read on to find out how cells make new cells.

MAKING CELLS

Every organism begins life as one cell. But how does one cell develop into trillions of others?

One way is by dividing and making identical copies of itself, a process known as **mitosis**. Here's how it works.

Original cell
DNA

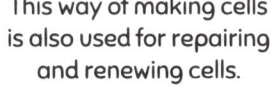
This way of making cells is also used for repairing and renewing cells.

Before dividing, a cell makes a copy of its DNA.

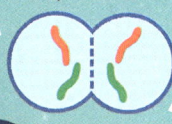

As the cell begins to divide, its DNA separates.

The cell divides into two identical cells, each with a full set of DNA – the same as the original cell.

As the process continues, two cells divide to make four cells, four cells divide to make eight, 16, 32, 64, 128 and so on.

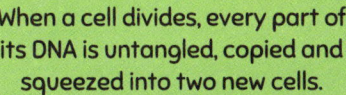

When a cell divides, every part of its DNA is untangled, copied and squeezed into two new cells.

Sounds fiddly. Does it ever go wrong?

Actually YES. Sometimes, bits of DNA are copied twice, or not at all, and the new cell is just a tiny little bit different from the original one.

Oh no!

Ah, but this is not always a bad thing. In fact, there's another way of making new cells. Turn the page to find out more.

37

SEX AND SEX CELLS

Another way of making new cells is to do with something called **sexual reproduction**, or sex. Biologists love studying it. This involves, among other things, DNA from two cells mingling and combining to create a new organism.

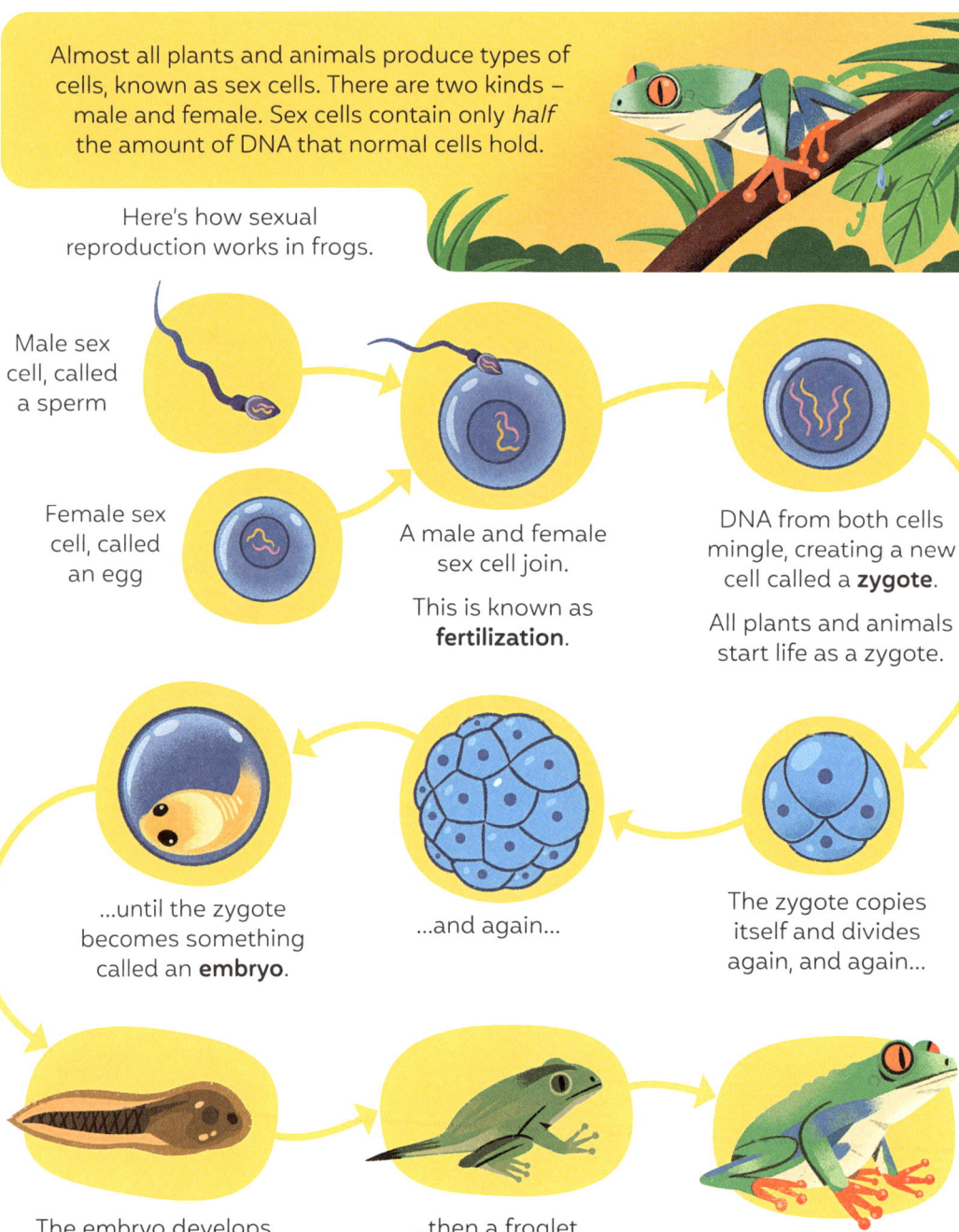

Almost all plants and animals produce types of cells, known as sex cells. There are two kinds – male and female. Sex cells contain only *half* the amount of DNA that normal cells hold.

Here's how sexual reproduction works in frogs.

Male sex cell, called a sperm

Female sex cell, called an egg

A male and female sex cell join.

This is known as **fertilization**.

DNA from both cells mingle, creating a new cell called a **zygote**.

All plants and animals start life as a zygote.

The zygote copies itself and divides again, and again...

...and again...

...until the zygote becomes something called an **embryo**.

The embryo develops into a tadpole...

...then a froglet with a tail...

...and finally a frog.

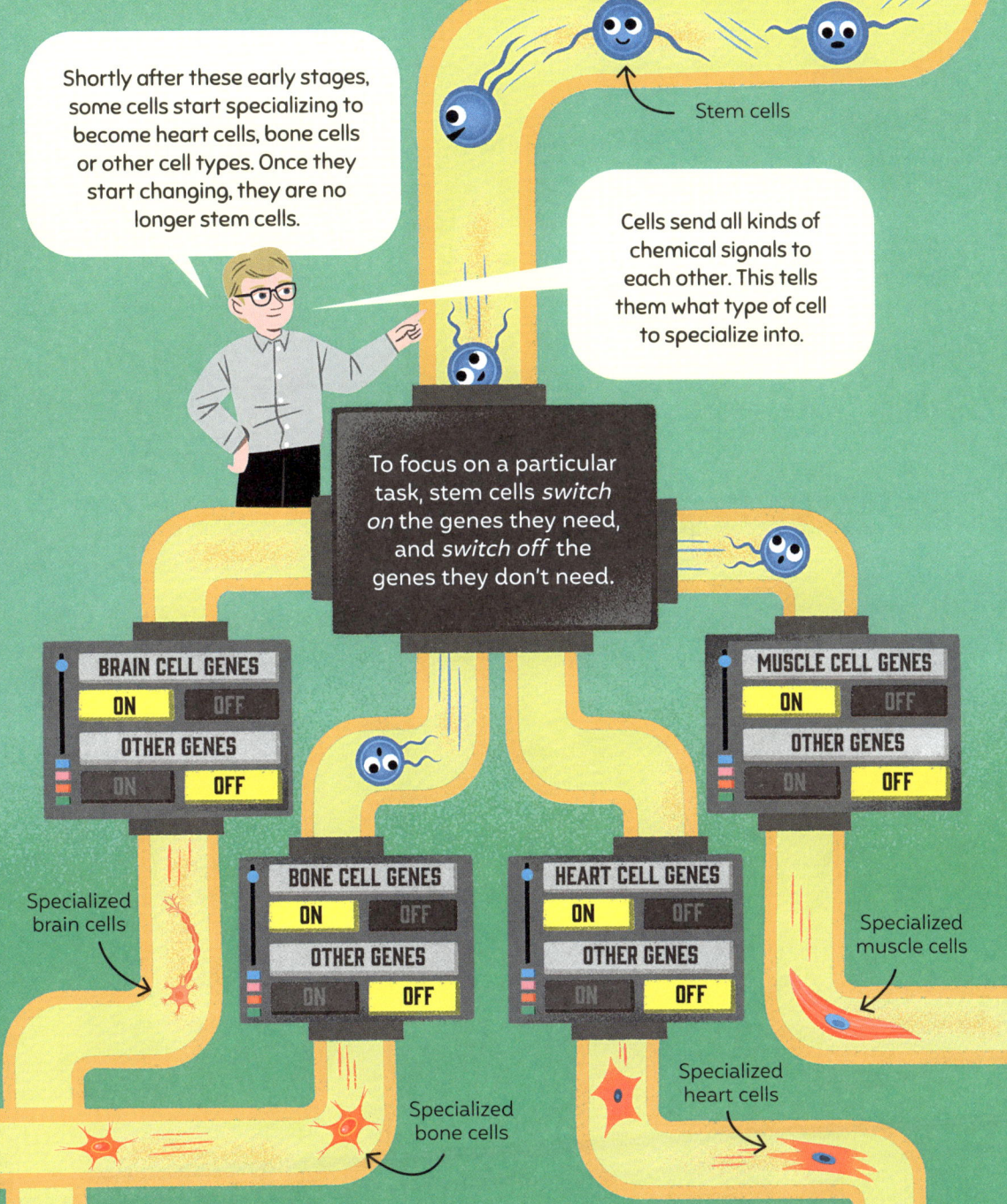

REGROWING BODY PARTS

Some animals use stem cells to grow back missing or damaged body parts. For example, salamanders regrow lost limbs and organs, while other animals can regrow their entire body from a tiny cut-off part.

Here's an axolotl – a type of salamander from Mexico. It can replace its legs, tail, skin, head – even its brain – thanks to stem cells.

After losing a foot, stem cells gather at the wound and divide speedily. They form a limb "bud" that makes a new foot in six weeks.

Sharks can replace lost teeth.

Deer shed and regrow their antlers every year.

They are the only mammals that can regenerate an organ.

Starfish can regrow arms, or their entire body from one cut-off arm.

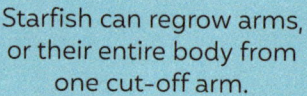

Will pangolins and humans ever be able to regrow body parts?

Biologists think it's only a matter of time! The animals above have a lot more stem cells. Scientists are looking at ways to turn stem cells into specialized cells that grow into any kind of animal tissue.

GENETIC ENGINEERING

It's not just stem cells that scientists are adapting. Some biologists are learning to rewrite an organism's DNA. This is part of a technology called **genetic engineering**. Here's an example: removing a gene from one organism and inserting it into another, to give it a new ability.

There's a gene in some jellyfish that makes them glow. Biologists can remove this gene...

...and insert it into a bacterium. The bacterium then lights up.

Cool! But is there any point to doing things like this?

I can use a similar method to make a treatment for diabetes. Read on...

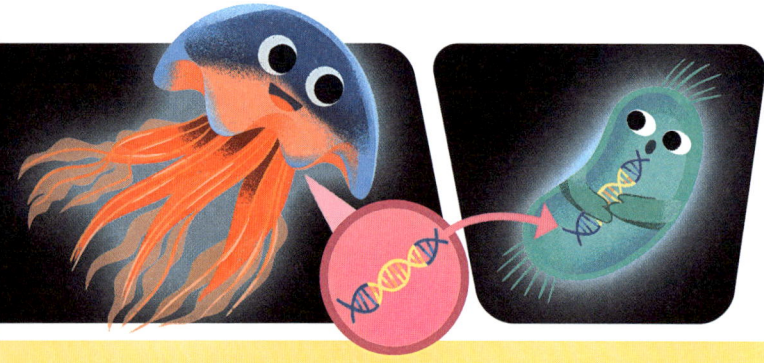

Many people with diabetes need to take insulin, a hormone that controls blood sugar levels. Biologists can remove the gene for making insulin from human DNA...

...and insert it in a plasmid – a circular DNA molecule that's found in bacteria.

The plasmid containing human insulin is then inserted into bacteria.

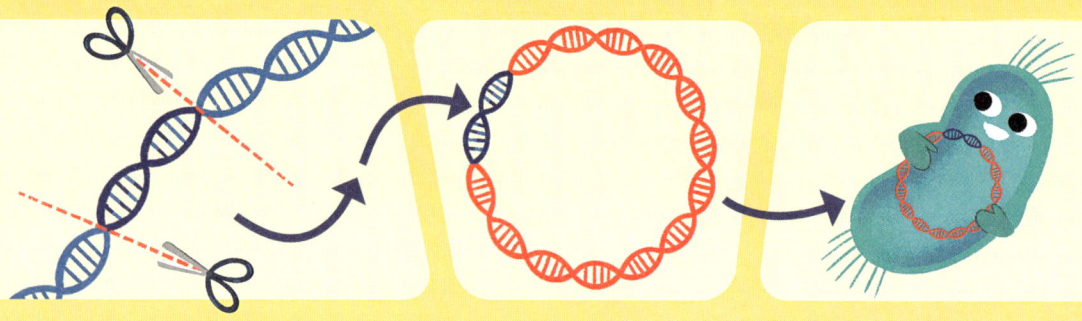

These bacteria reproduce rapidly in a lab, making human insulin. This is in huge demand around the world to treat diabetes.

Bacteria reproduction

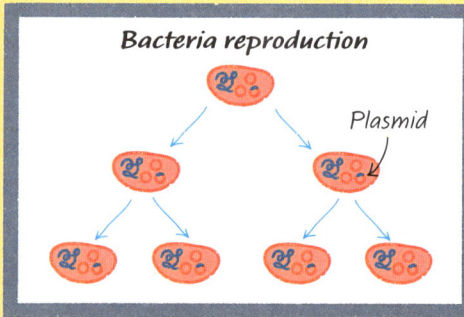

Plasmid

BIGGER, STRONGER, TASTIER, MORE

One of the oldest tricks genetic engineers have tried is changing plant DNA so that farmers can grow more and better food to eat. Here's how.

Farmers dream of crops that...

...produce lots of fruit

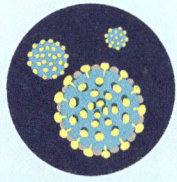
...are resistant to disease

...are resistant to drought or flooding

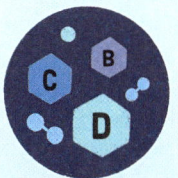
...are high in vitamins and nutrients

Genetic engineers can transfer genes with these qualities from plants into bacteria or viruses. These are then inserted into plant cells that grow into genetically modified (GM) plants. Their seeds have all the desired traits.

These GM crops are great! The corn is bigger, I grow more and it sells for more money. Why isn't everyone growing GM food?

GM crops make more food and could solve the problem of feeding the world. But we still don't know their long-term effects on the environment.

What kind of effects?

Disease-resistant crops can lead to disease-resistant weeds and new super bacteria that resist antibiotics. They also result in fewer insects, which harms biodiversity. And stronger GM crops soon overrun weaker ones, leading to less crop variety.

Hmm, insects are essential for pollination and variety is good. We don't want all our corn and tomatoes to taste the same.

SOLVING CRIMES

One of the most surprising things about human cells is how much information you can get from just a teaspoonful of them – even enough to solve a crime.

Here's the scene of a murder. There's evidence all over the place, hidden in the skin, hair and blood cells left behind by the people involved.

Forensic investigators are examining objects the culprits may have touched.

I can use a vacuum method to suck up all the DNA material left on this door handle.

This receipt may have dropped from a criminal's pocket.

Any touched object has a **fingerprint**, or residue, made up of sweat, oils and dead skin cells which all contain DNA. Investigators can detect these fingerprints and take samples of them.

The samples get sent to a lab. Forensic scientists extract DNA from them.

Then they perform a series of tests to find unique DNA belonging to one person. This is called a DNA profile.

Although everyone's DNA is similar, some sections of it are distinct for each indiviudal.

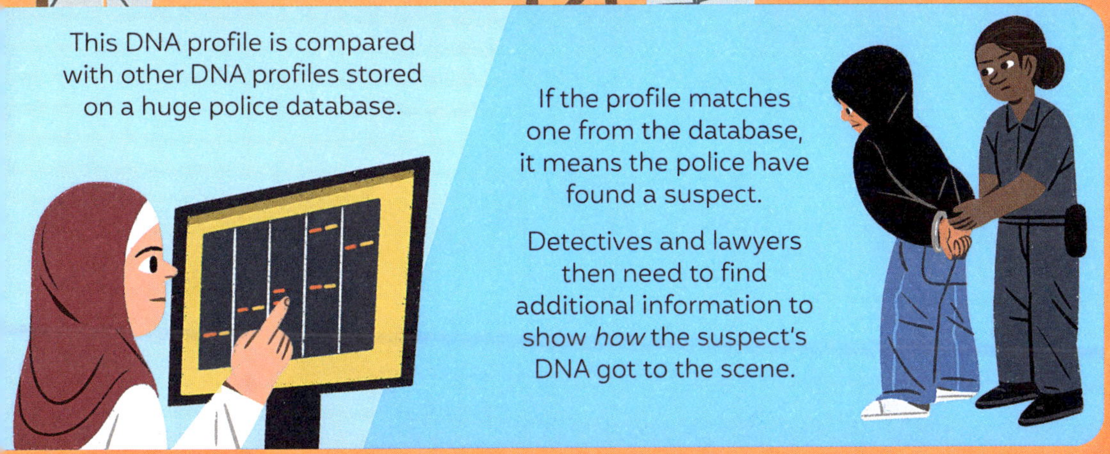

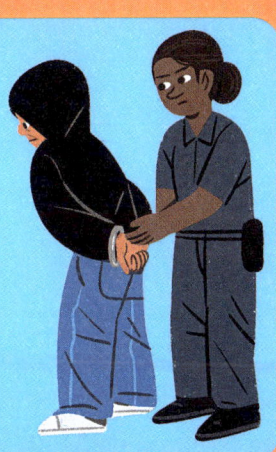

CHAPTER 3
EVOLUTION

Life on Earth is constantly changing. Most scientists agree that every species that's ever lived developed from earlier life forms over a long, long time. This process is known as evolution.

Evolution is one of biology's most important theories. It helps explain how life developed from the earliest cells, why there are so many different types of living things today, and how different species are related to each other.

Investigating the way organisms evolve helps biologists understand how new species are created. It also helps them find out how organisms are able to adapt to extreme environments and why some unlucky species die out altogether.

NATURAL SELECTION

A huge question in biology is "how do organisms evolve?" Most scientists agree that evolution is driven by a process called **natural selection**. This is how it works.

STAGE 1: EVERY LIFE IS UNIQUE

Most individuals in a species have slightly different characteristics – called **traits** – from one to the next. This is known as **variation**.

Take these veiled chameleons for example. They're all in the same species. Each has scaly skin and a curly tail, but they have some differences too.

Spiky back

Bigger head

Smaller body

Longer tongue

Where do those variations come from?

They're caused by tiny differences in each organism's DNA.

When two organisms reproduce with each other, they **mix** their DNA. Their offspring have a combination of traits from both parents.

Trait: smaller body

Trait: spiky back

Traits: smaller body, spiky back and...

...leaf-patterned skin

Every so often, random changes called **mutations** also creep into the DNA instructions.

Some types of mutation might cause problems. Others have no effect. Some turn out to be useful.

STAGE 2: GAINING AN ADVANTAGE

Certain traits might give an organism an advantage over other organisms in the same species.

My skin blends in with the bushes. Hehe!

Mine doesn't! Gulp.

Leaf-patterned skin helps this ONE chameleon to hide from predators – and survive for longer.

Chameleons without this trait might not be so lucky.

STAGE 3: PASSING ON TRAITS

Only the organisms that manage to survive go on to reproduce. When this happens, their offspring **inherit** their advantages. This is natural selection.

Natural selection means that the most useful traits get passed down to new generations.

See the ways my ancestors have changed over time. Thanks to them, I have a tail that helps me climb, and a hood on my head for collecting water.

These traits gradually become more common throughout the entire population – and the species evolves.

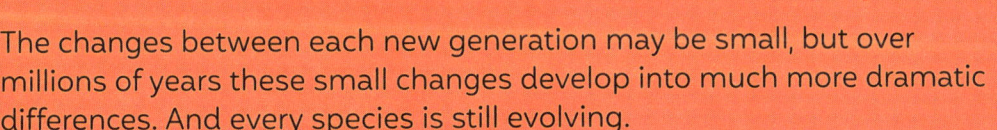

The changes between each new generation may be small, but over millions of years these small changes develop into much more dramatic differences. And every species is still evolving.

DARWIN'S VOYAGE

The theory of natural selection was first developed about 200 years ago by a British naturalist called Charles Darwin. He came up with it after sailing to South America on a voyage of scientific discovery.

One of the places Darwin visited was the Galápagos islands – a group of islands off the coast of Ecuador. Here, Darwin noticed that there were many similar species on each island – but all with different traits.

In the years after his return, Darwin developed a theory that explained the differences in the finches' beaks. He called it **evolution by natural selection**. Here's what he thought happened...

Long ago, all the finches lived on the mainland in South America. They all had similar beaks.

Gradually, some of the finches settled on separate islands. Different parts of each island had different sources of food.

South America

GALÁPAGOS ISLANDS

Insects

Large seeds

Cacti

Over many generations, the finches' beaks evolved to become better suited to eat the food available where they lived.

After many years of evolution, the finches changed so much that they became what scientists define as completely separate species.

My beak is great for crunching seeds.

Finch from the mainland

My beak can reach inside cactus fruits.

Large ground finch

Common cactus finch

So the finches that were best suited to their surroundings were the ones to survive and reproduce.

I believe that ALL living things evolve to adapt to their surroundings in one way or another. But I fear not everyone will agree with me.

51

BUILDING A CASE

Darwin didn't share his theory right away. He spent years gathering evidence to back up his big idea. With each new piece of evidence, it became more and more convincing.

These mammals live in different environments, but they all have similar bone structures with five fingers.

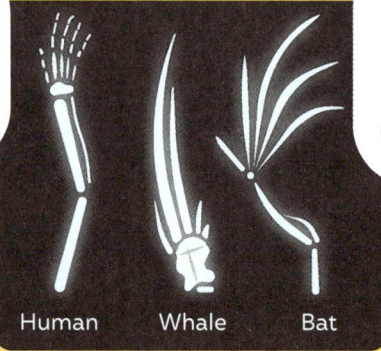
Human Whale Bat

This suggests that they once had a common ancestor. But over millions of years they evolved separately and adapted for different purposes.

Fossils helped to show how evolution happened. A particularly important fossil was of a 150 million-year-old creature called *Archaeopteryx*. Here's how it might have looked when it was alive.

Bird beak with reptile teeth

Reptile tail with bird feathers

Bird wings with reptile claws

Archaeopteryx has traits of both a reptile and a bird. This suggests that birds could have developed from older dinosaurs.

There are even signs of evolution in the human body, such as the tailbone at the base of the spine. Many mammals have this bone.

The fact that humans have a tailbone suggests we share a common ancestor with mammals that have tails.

In 1859, Darwin published his findings in a groundbreaking book called *On the Origin of Species*. It was controversial, because it challenged people's views about the foundations of life itself. In particular, it angered many (though not all) Christians. But Darwin had plenty of defenders too.

Life is so complex and diverse. Surely it must have been designed by a powerful creator, such as God.

I disagree. Natural selection explains how complicated organisms can develop through small changes over time.

Take the human eye for example. How can something so intricate have developed on its own?

In nature there are all sorts of eyes with different levels of complexity. Some are just simple, light-sensitive cells. This suggests that eyes like ours don't necessarily come fully formed.

So you're saying that every living thing evolved by some random chance? What tosh!

Natural selection isn't random. It's a process of change driven by the pressures of the environment and the fight for survival. Organisms adapt, or they die.

I still believe that God created us for a purpose. Our lives have got to have some sort of meaning.

But Darwin's theory isn't anything to do with God. Natural selection doesn't explain the origins of life, or its meaning – just how life on Earth has developed and is still evolving. The evidence is overwhelming.

ADAPT OR DIE

Today, biologists look for clues about why some species adapt and others don't. There are all sorts of pressures that might affect the way a species evolves.

Organisms need to adapt to the conditions of the **environment** they live in, including temperature, seasons and the climate.

Cacti have large, fleshy stems and prickly spines that help them store water in dry desert conditions.

Giant squid have developed enormous eyes that help them see their prey in the deep, dark ocean.

As well as evolving helpful physical traits, many species adapt the way they **behave**.

We're geese. Each winter, we fly south in search of warmer weather and more food. This type of journey is called **migration**.

As cities grow, and food gets more scarce, we've adapted to eat junk food that people leave behind.

If an environment keeps changing, the species that live there have to keep on adapting to survive.

Organisms that live in the same place also have to **compete** with each other for food and space. For example, both lions and cheetahs live in the African grasslands where they hunt different types of antelopes.

Lions are big and powerful, and they've evolved to hunt in groups. This means they can take down large antelope, such as wildebeest.

Aieee!! Not the claws!

Cheetahs are smaller than lions but they're faster too. So they hunt smaller, more agile creatures called impalas.

These different adaptations mean the two species avoid competing too much – so both survive.

If a species can't adapt or successfully compete, it becomes **extinct** – it dies out altogether.

Megatherium was an elephant-sized ground sloth. It went extinct around 10,000 years ago.

Megatherium may have lost its habitat because the climate was getting warmer. This probably meant it had to compete with other animals for a dwindling supply of food – but it couldn't adapt fast enough.

EVOLVING TOGETHER

Sometimes, when different species interact, they adapt in response to each other. This is known as **co-evolution**.

Co-evolution can happen between a predator species and its prey. Take these stone crabs and sea snails for example...

The crabs like to eat the sea snails. They use their claws to break into the snails' shells.

In response, the snails have evolved thick, spiny shells that are harder to break.

So in turn, the crabs have developed more powerful claws to break through the shells.

So the shells have become more spiny...

CRRRACK! SNAP!

ARRRGH!

...and the claws have got bigger. The evolutionary race continues.

You'll never defeat me. I'll just come back bigger and better.

Oh yeah? Try breaking through THIS!

Co-evolution can also happen when two species adapt to help each other out. This is known as **mutualism**.

Acacia ants live in whistling thorn acacia trees. The trees' branches have developed hollow, ball-shaped structures that the ants can live inside.

In return, the ants have evolved to be highly aggressive. They act as the trees' bodyguards, biting any leaf-eating animals.

SNAP!

Ouch!

Another clever form of co-evolution is **mimicry** – where one species evolves to look like another.

One of these is a highly venomous coral snake. The other is a harmless milk snake. Can YOU tell the difference?

Ummm...

Copying the coral snake's markings helps the milk snake warn off raccoons and other predators that want to eat it. This is because it looks more dangerous than it really is. (The milk snake is the one on the left.)

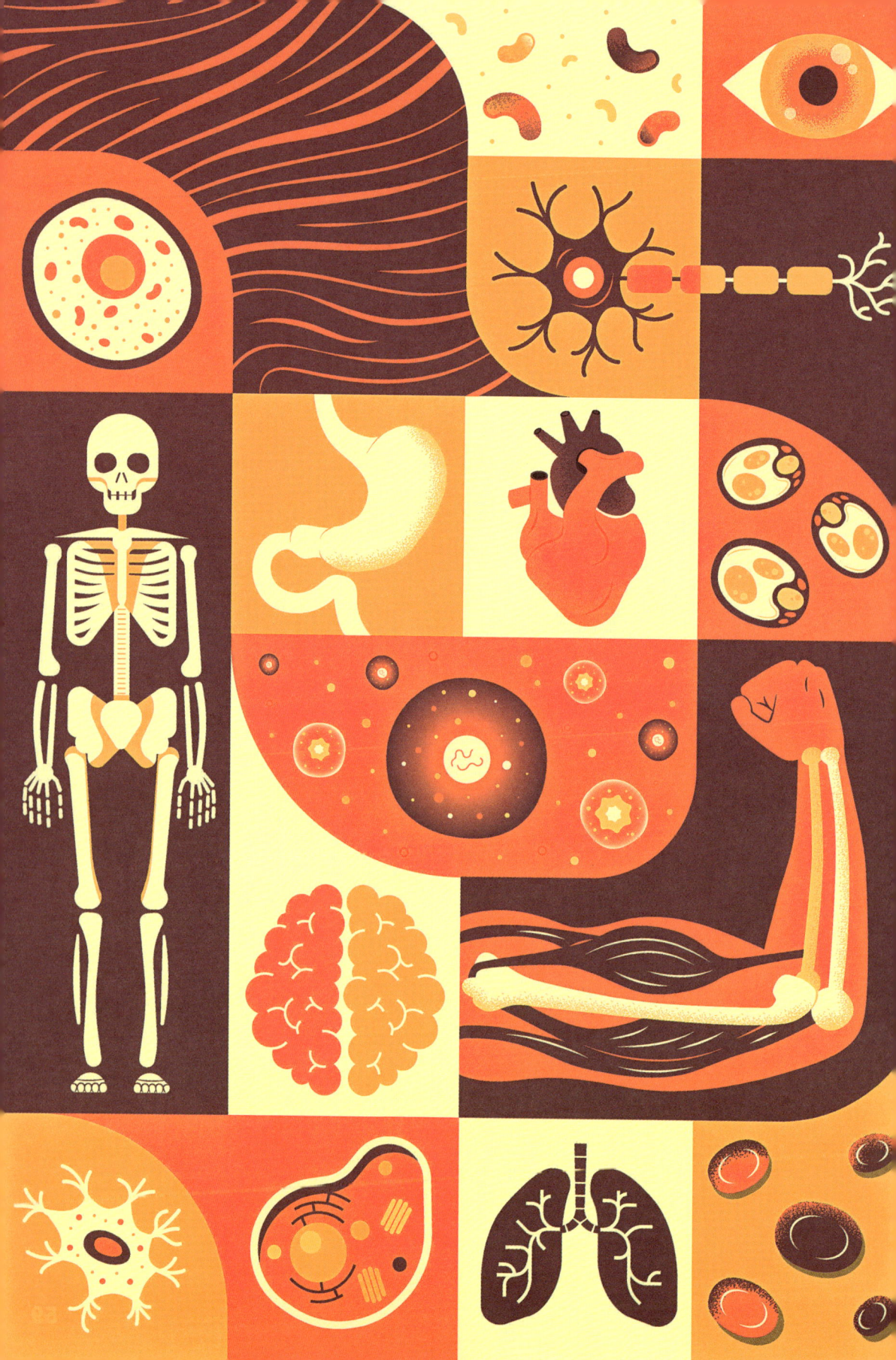

CHAPTER 4
THE HUMAN BODY

Recent advances in technology have allowed biologists to study the human body in incredible detail, and begin to answer all sorts of questions.

How does your brain control your body? Can the bacteria in your gut affect your mood? How unique is your DNA?

By understanding how the body works, scientists have been able to develop new medical procedures that can help people live longer, healthier lives.

LOOKING INSIDE THE BODY

One of the most fundamental things biologists study is **anatomy** – the structure of the body and everything in it, from the heart and lungs to muscles and bones. Here's a quick history lesson.

In the 1500s, a Belgian scientist called Andreas Vesalius was one of the first to make detailed observations about human anatomy through **dissection** – he cut open corpses to see what was inside.

Vesalius also educated others by performing dissections in public.

Behold – the human heart! See its structure, with four separate chambers.

Modern technology allows scientists today to see inside the bodies of living people, *without* cutting them open. One way of doing this is through a technique called Magnetic Resonance Imaging (MRI).

Inside an MRI scanner, a magnetic field works with radio waves to produce incredibly detailed images.

Like X-rays, it shows bones, but MRI also shows soft parts, including tissues, organs and even the brain.

MRI images are often used by doctors to detect different diseases in patients.

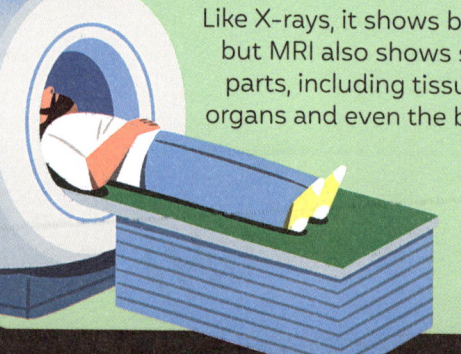
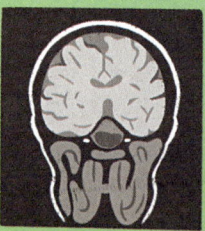

In recent years, scientists have used images from MRI scans to create digital 3D models of the body that can be viewed from different angles.

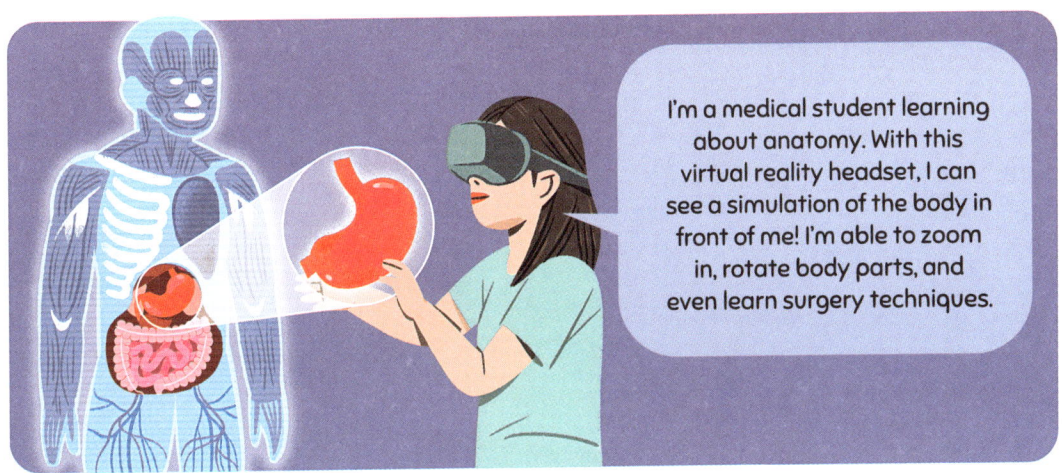

It's not just medical professionals who study human anatomy. An understanding of the body is useful in all sorts of jobs.

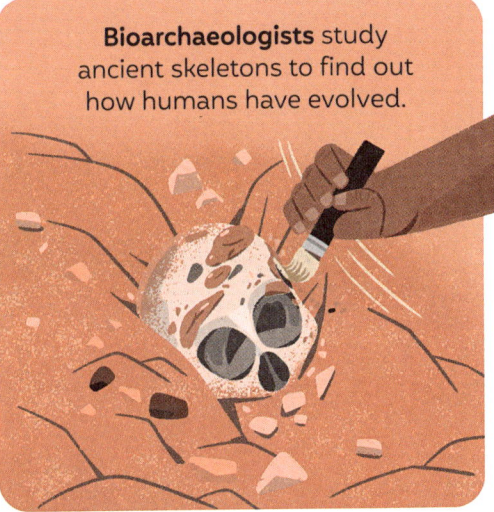

STAYING ALIVE

The human body is made up of organs, tissues, cells and chemicals that all do different things. They work together to handle the seven main processes that every organism needs for life (see page 8).

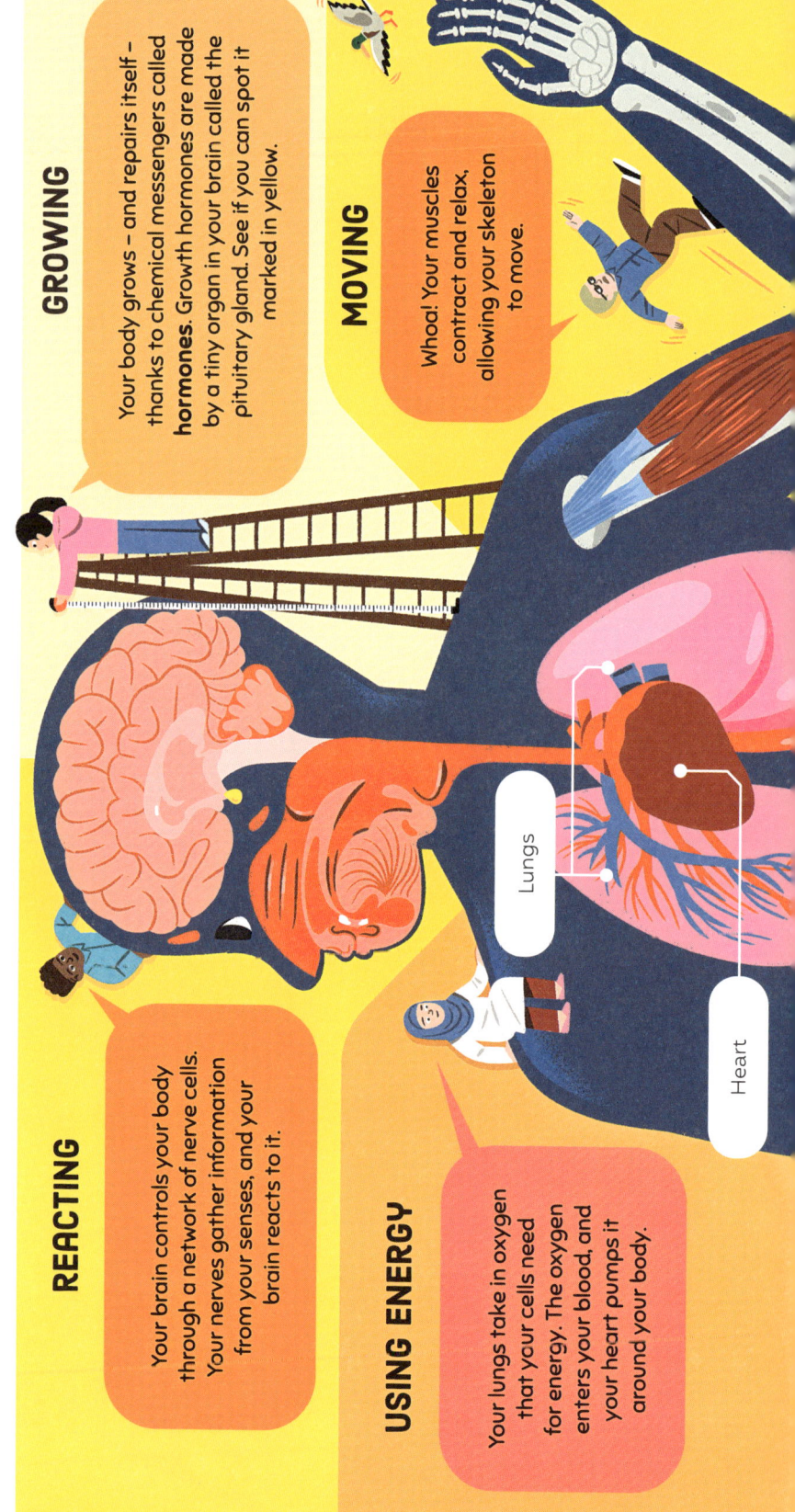

GROWING

Your body grows – and repairs itself – thanks to chemical messengers called **hormones**. Growth hormones are made by a tiny organ in your brain called the pituitary gland. See if you can spot it marked in yellow.

MOVING

Whoa! Your muscles contract and relax, allowing your skeleton to move.

REACTING

Your brain controls your body through a network of nerve cells. Your nerves gather information from your senses, and your brain reacts to it.

USING ENERGY

Your lungs take in oxygen that your cells need for energy. The oxygen enters your blood, and your heart pumps it around your body.

Lungs

Heart

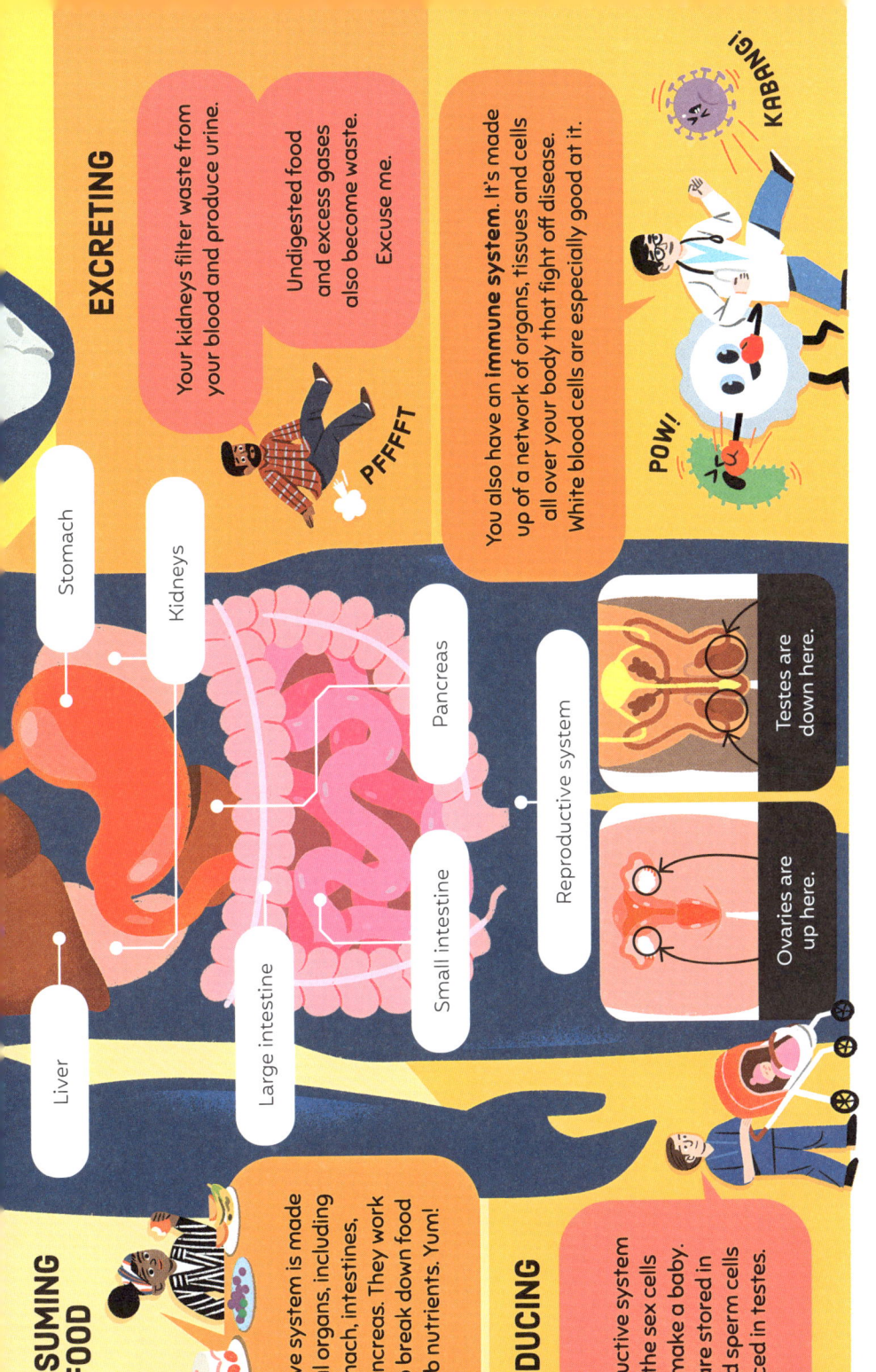

EXCRETING

Your kidneys filter waste from your blood and produce urine.

Undigested food and excess gases also become waste. Excuse me.

You also have an **immune system**. It's made up of a network of organs, tissues and cells all over your body that fight off disease. White blood cells are especially good at it.

CONSUMING FOOD

Your digestive system is made up of several organs, including your stomach, intestines, liver and pancreas. They work together to break down food and absorb nutrients. Yum!

- Liver
- Stomach
- Large intestine
- Kidneys
- Small intestine
- Pancreas
- Reproductive system

Ovaries are up here.

Testes are down here.

REPRODUCING

Your reproductive system produces the sex cells needed to make a baby. Egg cells are stored in ovaries and sperm cells are produced in testes.

The way different parts of the body function is called **physiology**. Human physiology is messy and complicated, and it varies from person to person. There's still a lot for biologists to discover, especially when it comes to the body's most complex organ – the brain. Turn the page to find out more.

THE BRAIN

The human brain may look like a ball of squashy stuff, but it's amazingly complex. It controls your whole body. People who study brains are called **neuroscientists**.

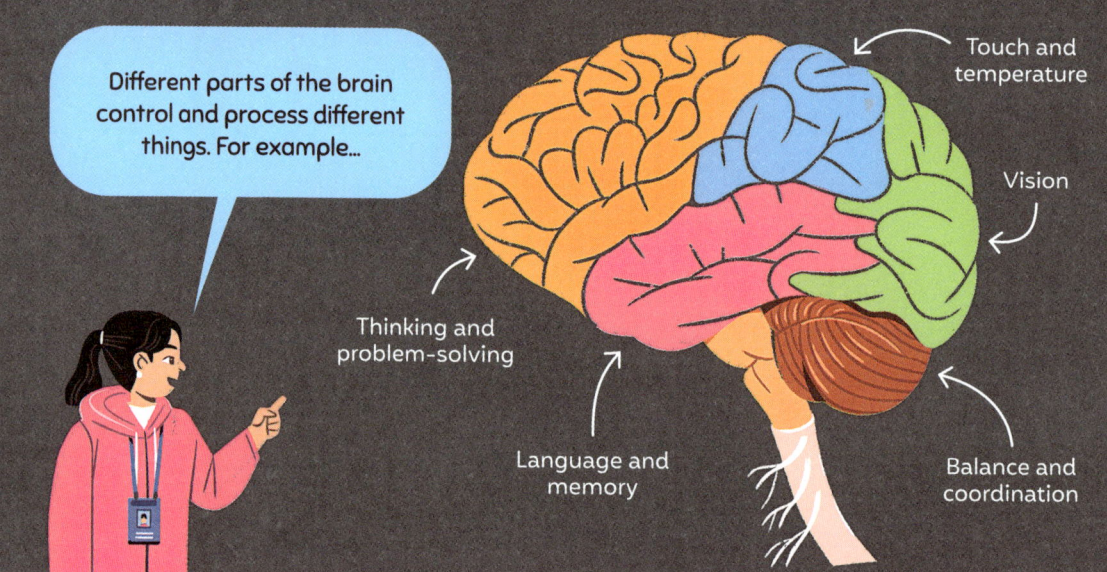

Different parts of the brain control and process different things. For example...

- Touch and temperature
- Vision
- Balance and coordination
- Language and memory
- Thinking and problem-solving

Your brain contains billions of cells called **neurons**. They send electrical and chemical signals to each other. If you decide to move your hand, your brain sends signals through your nerves to your muscles, telling them what to do.

When a signal is produced, it travels to the end of the neuron. It reaches a gap called a **synapse**, but it can't jump across...

...so the neuron releases chemical messengers called **neurotransmitters**. They cross the synaptic gap...

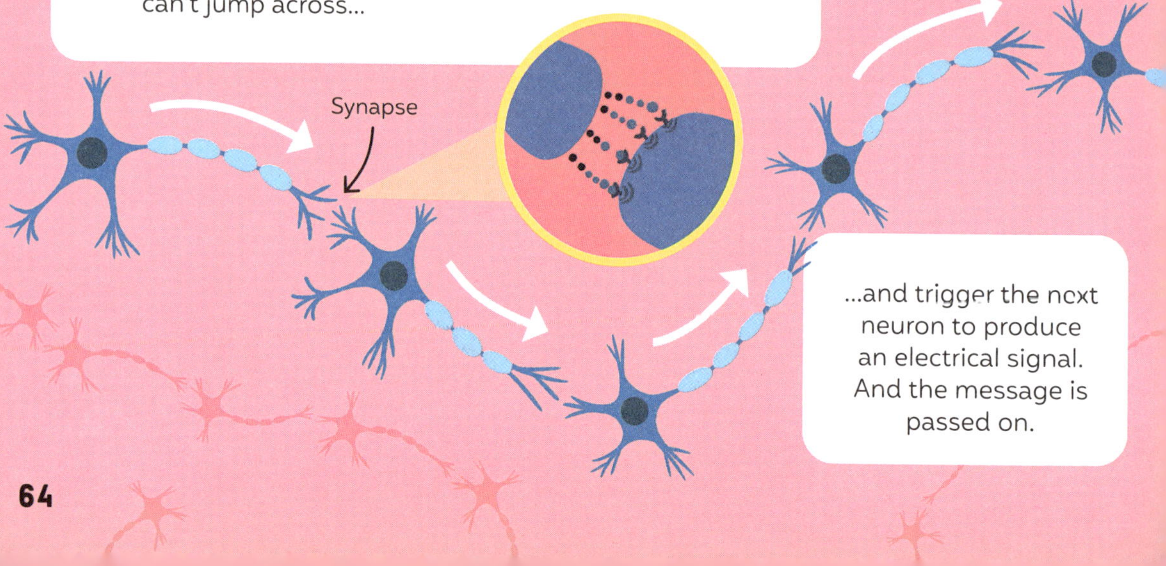

...and trigger the next neuron to produce an electrical signal. And the message is passed on.

Your brain processes information by creating complex **pathways** of neurons. It can also change and reorganize these pathways. This amazing ability is called **neuroplasticity**. It's what allows us to learn new things.

When you learn a new skill, your neurons set up all sorts of pathways. Rehearsing helps your brain test which pathway is best.

As you keep rehearsing, your brain uses the best pathway again and again. So the pathways become stronger and the skill becomes easier.

Most animal brains contain neurons and send signals, just like human brains. Neuroscientists are interested in finding out what makes human brains *different*.

In humans, the parts of the brain that handle complex functions are highly developed. These functions include problem-solving, language and memory.

That doesn't make you unique though. Many animals are highly intelligent – elephants have incredible memories. Crows can use tools to find food.

And we dolphins use a language of whistles and clicks to communicate. EEEE Ek-Ek-Ek!

Ek-Ek!

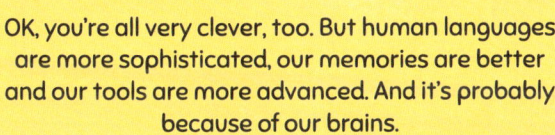

OK, you're all very clever, too. But human languages are more sophisticated, our memories are better and our tools are more advanced. And it's probably because of our brains.

BACTERIA IN YOUR BODY

Your body isn't just yours. It's home to trillions of bacteria living on your skin and inside different organs. One of the most useful groups are gut bacteria that live in your digestive system.

Biologists have discovered that each person has a unique combination of bacteria in their gut – usually around 300-500 types. Together they make up something called your **gut microbiome**.

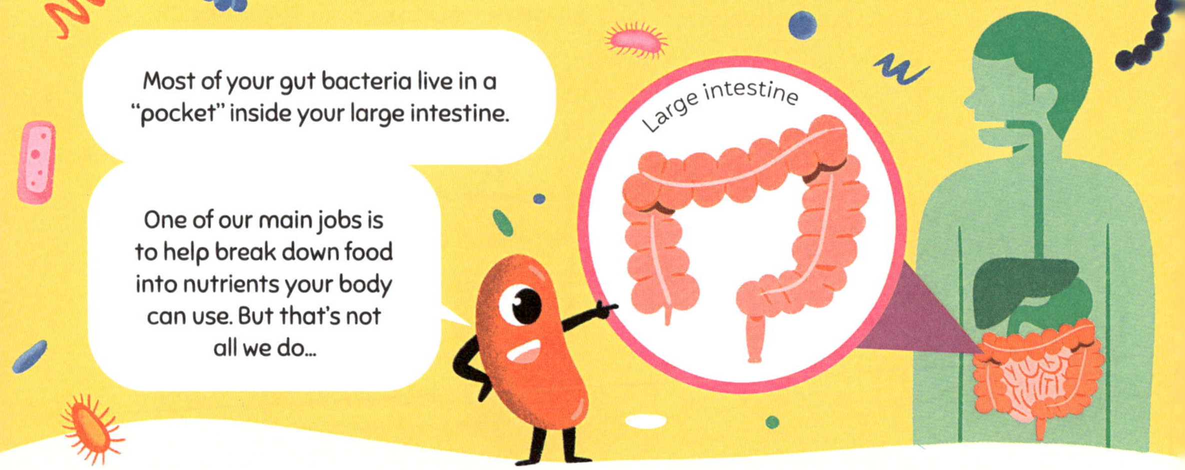

Most of your gut bacteria live in a "pocket" inside your large intestine.

One of our main jobs is to help break down food into nutrients your body can use. But that's not all we do...

Scientists have discovered that your microbiome can have a huge impact on your health. It helps protect you from infection and disease.

Your gut bacteria help train your white blood cells to tell the difference between good bacteria and bad ones.

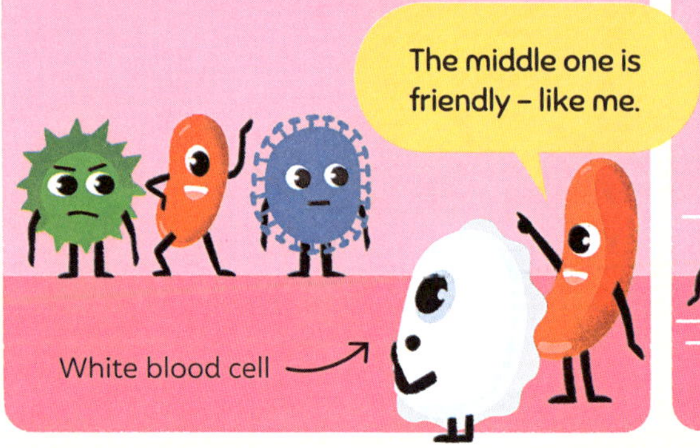

The middle one is friendly – like me.

White blood cell

Good bacteria also act as a barrier against harmful microorganisms by crowding them out, and producing chemicals that stop them from developing.

Get out of here!

Biologists are particularly interested in the relationship between your gut microbiome and your brain. They're connected directly by a nerve – called the vagus nerve – which allows them to communicate easily.

Understanding the links between the gut and the brain can help scientists come up with more effective treatments for all sorts of problems. This can be anything from issues with digestion to mental illnesses.

THE HUMAN GENOME

To find out what makes up the human body at the most fundamental level, biologists study a complete set of instructions encoded in our DNA. This is known as the **human genome**.

DNA contains four main chemicals – adenine (A), cytosine (C), thymine (T) and guanine (G). They're known as **bases** and they form pairs along each DNA strand.

The outer edge is made of sugars and other chemicals.

The **base pairs** are organized into a precise sequence, like steps in an instruction manual.

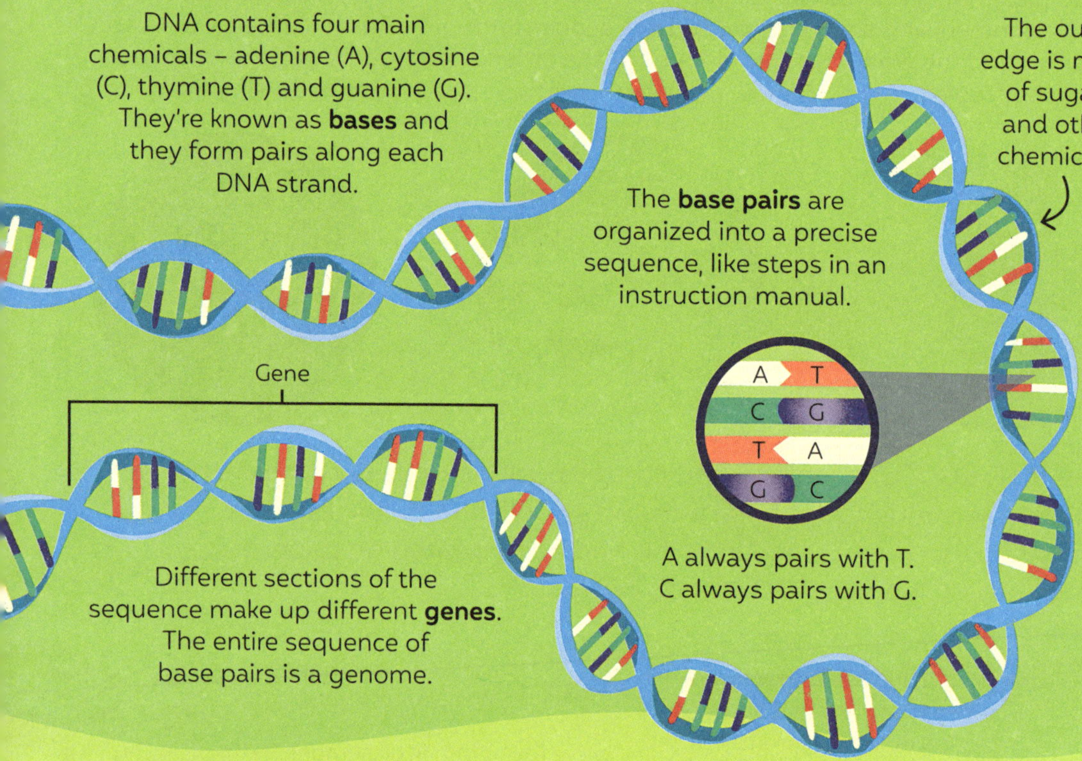

Gene

Different sections of the sequence make up different **genes**. The entire sequence of base pairs is a genome.

A always pairs with T.
C always pairs with G.

All living things have a genome. There's a copy of it in most of their cells. Organisms in the same species all have very similar genomes to each other.

A duck genome has around 1 billion base pairs.

A pangolin genome has around 2.5 billion base pairs.

A human genome has around 3 billion base pairs. But just how similar is one human's genome to the next? Scientists wondered this for years. Until...

THE HUMAN GENOME PROJECT

In 1990, scientists set up a project to figure out the order of all 3 billion base pairs in the human genome. It was the world's largest collaboration of biologists, and was called the Human Genome Project.

DNA samples were gathered from 20 volunteers and sent to labs around the world to be studied.

Scientists used a process called **DNA sequencing** to determine the order of the base pairs.

They compared sections of the volunteers' DNA and combined the information, to create a single sequence.

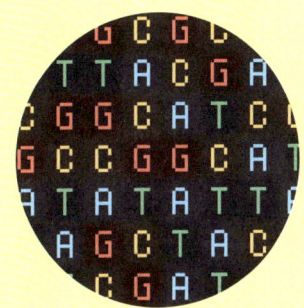

By the early 2000s, scientists had come up with a draft of the human genome. The sequence of base pairs was published online for other scientists to use in their research. If it had been printed on paper, it would have filled over 10,000 books.

> How can there be a single sequence for every human? You all look different.

> We've found that in all humans, 99.9% of our genome is identical. There's just 0.1% genetic variation that determines our unique traits, such as my long nose and super curly hair.

> So could you use this sequence to build a brand new human?

> In theory, yes. But it would be incredibly difficult to do in reality. And it would raise all sorts of ethical issues, too.

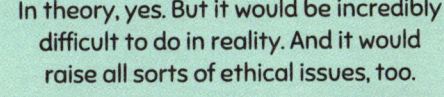

CHAPTER 5
ECOLOGY

Ecology is about how living things, including humans, interact with their environment.

From coral reefs and rainforests to cities and rivers, ecologists look at how and why environments are changing and the effect of those changes on different organisms.

Why are crocodiles dying in Australia? How do scientists track narwhals under Arctic ice? Why is the world's biggest and stinkiest flower becoming extinct?
To find answers to questions like these, ecologists gather lots of information, or data. They also look for solutions.

COASTAL HABITATS

As the world heats up, ice is melting and sea levels are rising. This is washing away the nesting sites of thousands of turtles and birds. High temperatures also directly affect turtle numbers. Here's how…

CASE STUDY: SEA TURTLES

Every two or three years, sea turtles swim back to the same beach they hatched on to lay their eggs. They dig a hole in the sand and bury their eggs above the level of high tide, to guard against flooding.

Temperature is key to turtles' survival because it determines the sex of hatchlings. Temperatures above 31°C (87.8°F) produce females, below 27.7°C (81.9°F), males. Between that, a mixture.

Soaring heat can also "cook" the eggs, destroying the embryos inside. Hot weather means fewer male turtles and fewer hatchlings.

No gulls ahead – quick, let's go!

Leatherback turtle eggs hatch after 50-60 days. The hatchlings crawl out of the sand and race to the sea.

Ecologists are using global mapping technology to predict which turtle beaches are most at risk. Then, they go to those beaches and look for turtle tracks that lead them to nests: shallow pits with thrown sand.

We're building a shade over these nests. We're also going to split up some eggs from the clutches. Both tricks will help keep eggs cooler.

ECOLOGY AND CLIMATE CHANGE

Many ecologists see global warming as the single biggest threat to habitats and the organisms that live there.

HABITAT CASE STUDY: CORAL REEFS

Coral reefs make up only 1% of marine habitats but are home to about 25% of all sea life, including turtles, rays, crabs, squid, octopus, sponges, whales, dolphins and over 6,000 species of fish.

Coral is made up of animals that secrete a hard substance that looks like rock. Coral looks bright because of tiny algae, called **zooxanthellae**, that live inside it.

Coral reefs provide sheltered areas, where sea creatures feed, hide, give birth and care for their young.

Coral and algae depend on each other to survive. The algae pass energy from the Sun to coral cells, and the algae gain nutrients and shelter from the coral.

A warming planet means warming oceans. This threatens coral reefs – and the huge range of life they support – because they're highly sensitive to changes in temperature.

CORAL IN CRISIS

An ocean temperature rise of just 1°C (2°F) over four weeks can trigger **coral bleaching**. This is when coral expels its algae, loses its bright shades and turns white.

Bleached coral can still survive, sometimes for years. If the temperature returns to normal and the algae returns, coral can become healthy again. If not, the coral dies.

RESCUE MISSIONS

Ecologists are exploring many ways to restore and preserve coral reefs. Here are some projects ecologists are involved in.

Gathering broken coral and securing it to solid structures.

Once secured, coral can repair damaged tissue and regrow.

Regrowing coral in small pieces in labs where there's a steady temperature...

...then, when it's safe, transplanting the pieces back into reefs.

Gathering coral eggs and sperm.

About once a year, coral colonies release a mass of eggs and sperm into the ocean.

We gather eggs and sperm to develop genetically diverse coral species, including ones that can survive in warmer temperatures.

Sperm and eggs

75

PREDATOR INVASION

Counting the number, or **population**, of animals is one way to measure how ecologically healthy a region is. Animal populations can vary as a result of disease, habitat loss or drought. They also change when a new predator arrives. Here's an example.

SAVING SPECIES

There is no disease or predator in Australia that controls cane toad numbers. So, ecologists and local wildlife experts are working on new ways to protect animals from them.

Here's one solution for protecting freshwater crocodiles: training the crocodiles to avoid cane toads, so they don't die from poisoning.

Another solution is genetics.

Squirrel-sized marsupials called quolls have also been dying from eating cane toads. But one isolated group of quolls has evolved an aversion to cane toads. Scientists are using this group to breed new populations of quolls.

ECOLOGY TECHNOLOGY

New technology, such as audio sensors and DNA testing, is changing the way ecologists monitor natural habitats and the organisms that live there.

PEAT HABITATS

One example is peat. Peat is a kind of soil, made of dead and decaying organisms, that stores vast amounts of carbon. As a result, peat helps reduce global warming – good news for most living things.

Peat also provides a habitat for rare animals and plants. It reduces flooding, too, because it absorbs lots of water.

Once, people dug up peat to use as fuel, or drained water to turn peat areas into farmland. Conservationists are now *rewetting* and restoring them.

Low-power sensor systems monitor CO_2 gas emissions between peat and the air. So we can see if our project is working.

To monitor the population of water voles in this peat area, ecologists are taking water samples and using DNA testing to determine their presence.

I've spotted a water vole toilet area – piles of droppings flattened by their feet. This must be a good place to test for water voles!

ARCTIC EXPLORATION

As sea temperatures rise, Arctic glaciers and sea ice are melting. Ecologists are monitoring how this affects species that rely on the ice for their survival.

NARWHALS

Narwhals have long, spiralled tusks, or teeth. For almost half the year, they live under the ice between Canada and Greenland.

> Sea ice is key to narwhals' survival. How ice melts and retreats in the spring determines where narwhals hunt and give birth.

Ecologists studying narwhals use high-tech microphones to pick up the narwhals' calls.

By tracking their location, ecologists can see if their migration routes and way of life are changing.

POLAR BEARS

As Arctic ice decreases, polar bears are forced to spend more time on land, bringing them closer to people. This is dangerous for both bears and humans.

Ecologists are using new stick-on GPS tags, like this one, to track the bears.

The tags drop off after two months.

> Knowing the bears' location is crucial for understanding the way they behave, and keeping them safe.

FORESTS OF LIFE

Tropical rainforests provide a habitat for over 30 million species of animals, plants, fungi and microorganisms – including two thirds of Earth's plant species. That's why ecologists are desperate to conserve them.

Rainforests, like this one in Borneo, are home to all kinds of rare species, from orangutans and clouded leopards to slipper orchids and the giant rafflesia – the biggest flower in the world.

Slow loris

Orangutan

Sabah flying squirrel

Lantern fly

Animals and plants need each other to survive. This tree shrew needs nectar from the pitcher plant, and the plant needs nutrients from the shrew's dung.

Orchids

Pitcher plant

Tree shrew

Pitcher plant leaves make cups to collect dung and insects.

Banded palm civet

DEFORESTATION

In many forests, trees are disappearing fast to make space for farms, mines, buildings and roads. The vast majority of deforestation in the world takes place in tropical rainforests.

Cutting down rainforests reduces the habitat for thousands of endangered plants and animals, such as orangutans, pygmy elephants and Sumatran rhinos.

Losing the tree canopy can expose the land to extreme heat, increasing the likelihood of drought and wildfires.

After trees have been cut down, bulldozers and excavators move in. People use fire and chemicals to clear remaining plants and make space for farms or buildings.

WHAT IS BIODIVERSITY AND WHY IS IT IMPORTANT?

Biodiversity means having a wide range of living things and a wide range of habitats. It's essential for creating healthy air, clean water and food – and for the survival of life on Earth.

GREEN DESERTS

Vast palm oil farms are another major cause of deforestation. Palm oil comes from the fruit of oil palm trees and is used in many foods and products. Growing these trees also makes **green deserts**, where few native plants and animals can survive.

PALM OIL FARM

1. Farmers add fertilizers and pesticides to the land to increase plant yields.

2. Pesticides can kill pollinating insects, including bees. They also run into rivers, poisoning plants and fish.

3. Losing ground plants, fungi, roots and wildlife leads to soil erosion and reduces soil nutrients and fertility.

4. More and more fertilizers need to be added, harming plants and soil even more.

Is there a way to farm palm oil that's better for the environment?

Yes. Farmers can avoid harmful chemicals and grow low plants among the palm trees.

Big plantations that grow only one crop increase the risk of pests and disease. Instead, farmers can mix palm with other crops, such as beans or cocoa.

One job for biologists and ecologists is to find solutions. For instance, they're reforesting areas and helping farmers produce deforestation-free crops. They're also educating people to demand it.

ANIMAL AND PLANT LIBRARIES

Biologists are working on new ways to prevent total extinctions, using a special kind of library. But, the library has to be set up BEFORE a species has lost all of its individuals.

LIBRARY 1: FROZEN ZOOS

Biologists are gathering the genetic material – skin, sperm and egg cells – of thousands of threatened animal species. The cells are frozen in tanks of liquid nitrogen at -196°C (-321°F). They can be stored like this for centuries – and used to reproduce species artificially.

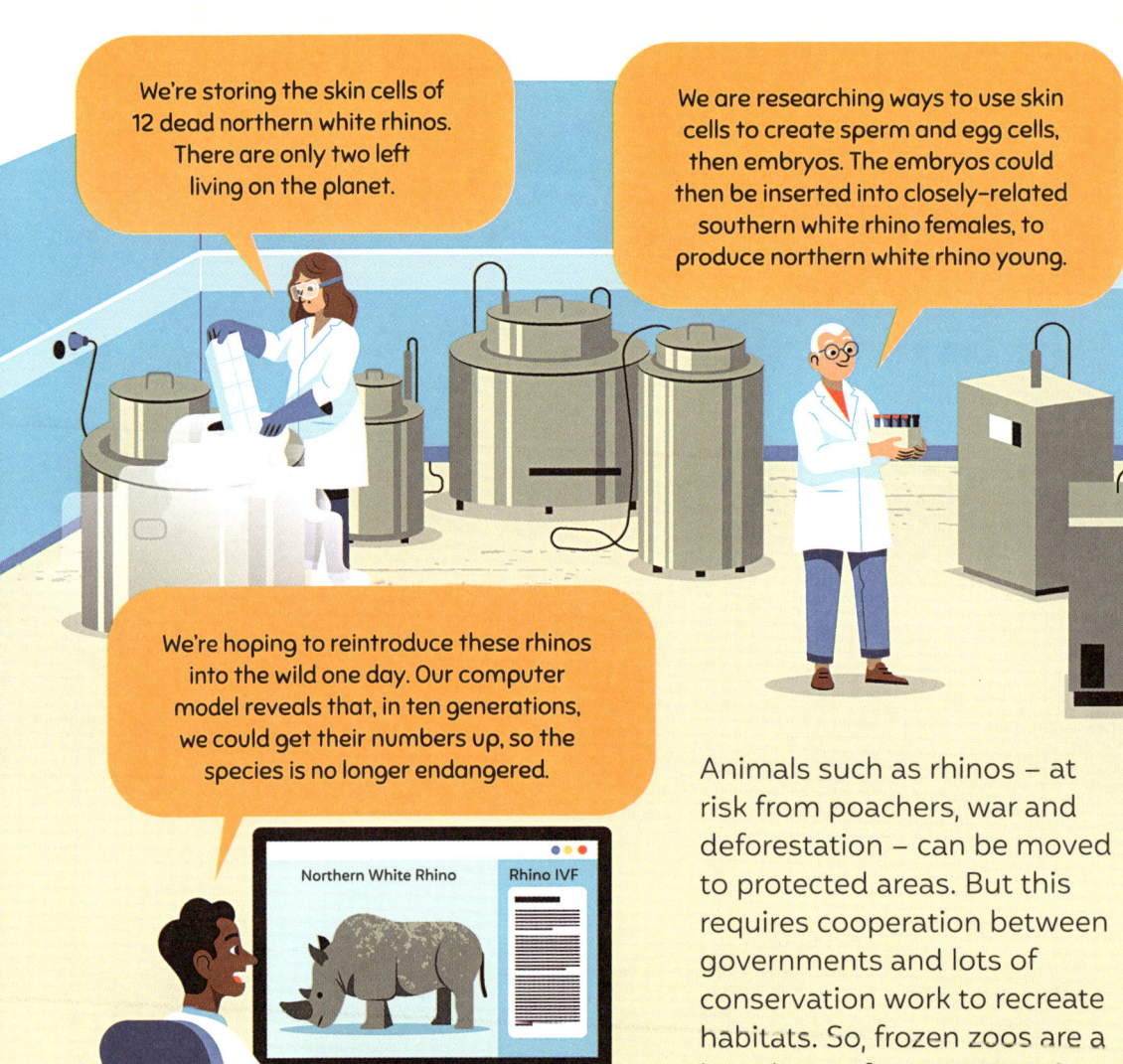

We're storing the skin cells of 12 dead northern white rhinos. There are only two left living on the planet.

We are researching ways to use skin cells to create sperm and egg cells, then embryos. The embryos could then be inserted into closely-related southern white rhino females, to produce northern white rhino young.

We're hoping to reintroduce these rhinos into the wild one day. Our computer model reveals that, in ten generations, we could get their numbers up, so the species is no longer endangered.

Animals such as rhinos – at risk from poachers, war and deforestation – can be moved to protected areas. But this requires cooperation between governments and lots of conservation work to recreate habitats. So, frozen zoos are a last chance for many species.

LIBRARY 2: SEED BANKS

Two in five plants are threatened with extinction. To save plant biodiversity and ensure a future food supply, biologists are creating banks of seeds from a wide variety of crops.

Seeds can be dried and sealed in water-resistant packets...

...then stored in airtight containers at cool temperatures.

Entrance to Svalbard Global Seed Vault

The world's biggest seed bank is located on Spitsbergen, a remote Norwegian island in the Arctic Ocean. It contains 6,000 different plant species from around the world and is built to withstand earthquakes and keep the seeds at a steady temperature of –18°C (–0.4°F).

Scientists are considering a seed bank and animal cell store on the Moon – called the Lunar Ark – to save Earth's biodiversity in case of a mass extinction event.

Great! So we don't need to worry about plants becoming extinct.

Wrong! Over a third of plants can't be stored by drying and freezing. Chestnuts, for instance, have a high water content and cannot be preserved this way. We need other ways to save them.

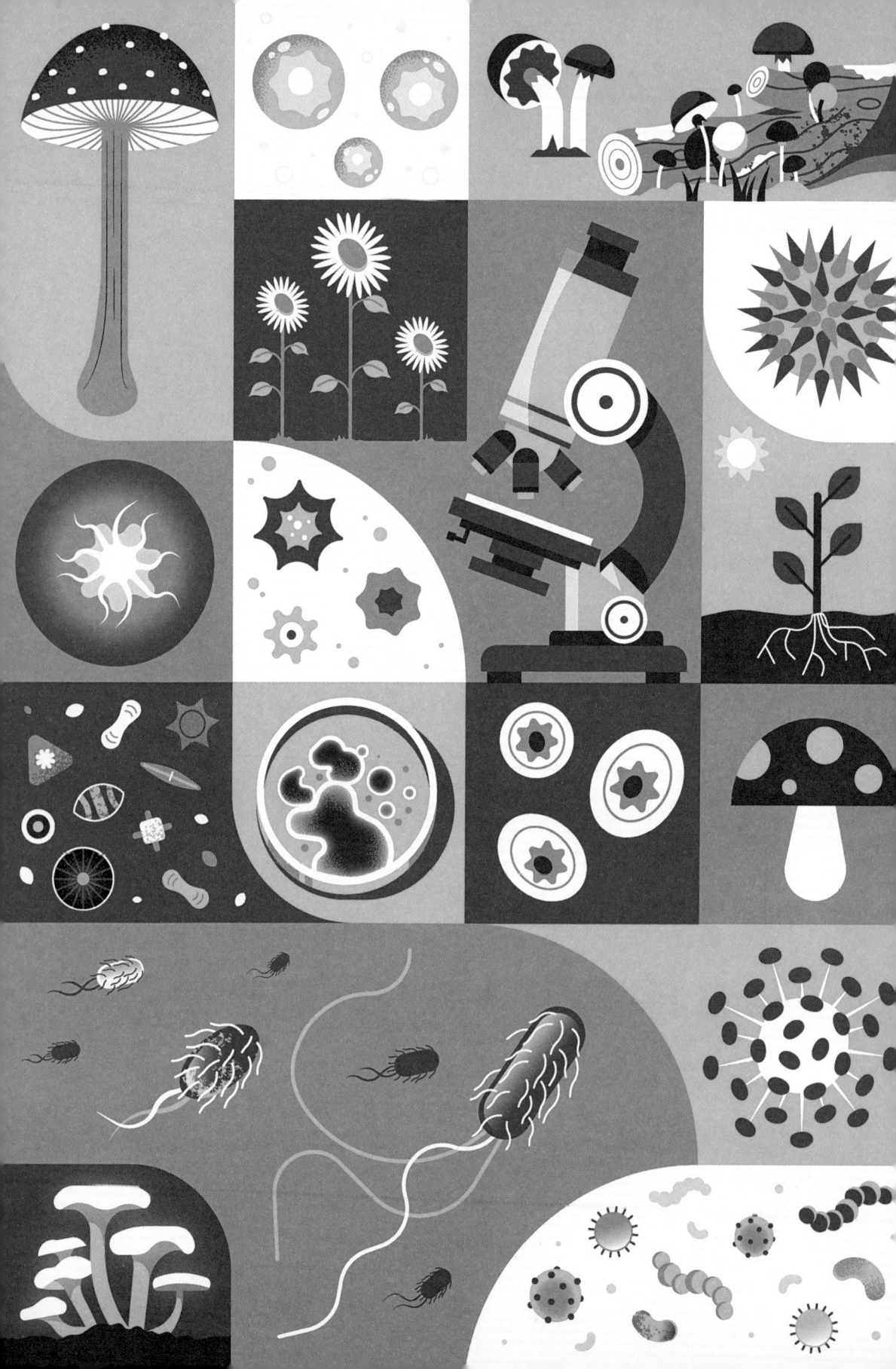

CHAPTER 6
MICROORGANISMS

Microorganisms, such as bacteria and fungi, are everywhere. They're essential for shaping the environment, whether by controlling the way nutrients move through soil or helping trees to talk to each other. Life on Earth wouldn't be possible without them.

By understanding how microorganisms work, biologists can also use them in all sorts of amazing ways, from producing foods and medicines to creating fuels that are more eco-friendly.

WHAT IF...

...there were no decomposers? Scientists were able to research this question following a disaster in 1986 – when a nuclear reactor exploded at a power plant in Chernobyl, Ukraine.

BOOOooM!

The explosion blasted out radiation that contaminated the surrounding area. It killed lots of organisms, including many trees and decomposers.

As pine trees in the nearby forest died, they turned red and their needles fell off. This area became known as the Red Forest.

30 years later, scientists studied the Red Forest. New trees had grown, but as radiation levels in the soil remained high, there were few decomposers.

Normally it takes pine needles 1–3 years to decay. But without the decomposers these needles are still here! Leaves from newer trees keep on piling up too.

The cycle of life is completely disrupted!

FANTASTIC FUNGI

While some types of fungi are great at breaking things down, others do different jobs that are just as important.

These mushrooms don't look like they're doing much.

The mushrooms are just the fruit of the fungus. Under the ground, there's so much more going on...

The underground part of a fungus is a tangle of root-like threads called **mycelium**.

In some types of fungi, the mycelium connects with the roots of trees and passes them nutrients. This is called a **mycorrhizal network**.

In return, the fungus gets some of the sugars made by the trees during photosynthesis.

The fungus also carries chemical signals between different trees. This allows the plants to warn each other of danger or disease.

Around 90% of all plants on the planet depend on mycorrhizal networks to survive.

Not all types of fungi are helpful to plants. Some types are **parasites** – that means they steal nutrients, which can weaken plants or even kill them.

These innocent-looking honey mushrooms rot the roots of trees. They're part of a *single* enormous parasitic fungus network.

It lives in Oregon, USA, and it covers an area the size of 1,800 football fields.

This network is nicknamed the Humongous Fungus. It's the biggest single organism on Earth, and it's still growing.

Some types of fungi have amazing properties which scientists think could even help tackle pollution caused by humans.

This mould can decompose certain kinds of plastic. Some types of bacteria can do this too.

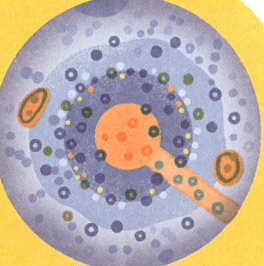

Aspergillus tubingensis

This yeast is able to break down and digest toxic compounds in oil spills.

Candida tropicalis

The mycelium of this fungus can be used to make eco-friendly fabrics, such as mushroom leather.

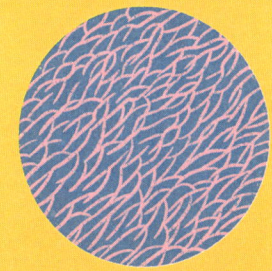

Ganoderma lucidum

Wow! Could we somehow use microorganisms to get rid of plastic pollution and clean up oil spills in the oceans?

So far it's only worked with tiny amounts of oil or plastic. The real challenge is figuring out how to make it work on a much bigger scale.

USEFUL MICROORGANISMS

Bacteria and fungi can be incredibly useful for making all sorts of things, from dairy products, bread and alcohol to medicines and fuels. It's done through a process called **fermentation**.

YOGURT-MAKING FOR BEGINNERS

Step 1.
First, add a strain of yogurt-making bacteria such as *Lactobacillus* to milk. This is called a starter culture.

Step 2.
Store the mixture in a fermentation tank. Here the bacteria break down some of the milk into a substance called **lactic acid**.

Step 3.
Wait for 8 hours. Lactic acid thickens the milk and turns it into yogurt.

The starter culture is usually taken from an older batch of milk or yogurt that's rich in bacteria. People have been using this method for thousands of years.

In recent years, scientists have used fermentation to develop new types of foods, such as mycoprotein.

This is a mycoprotein burger. Mycoprotein is a meat substitute made from fermented fungi. It takes less energy and land to produce than meat does.

These fermented foods have been around for centuries.

Microorganisms are used to make many antibiotics, medicines and vaccines. Fermentation is vital for producing these drugs on a large scale.

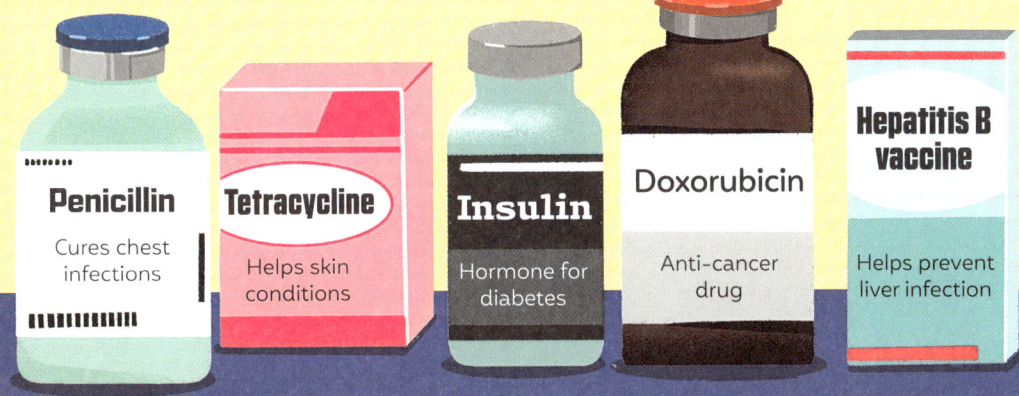

Some bacteria, such as *E. coli*, are used to produce cleaner fuels, called **biofuels**. Biofuels are made by fermenting crops, such as soybeans, to make methane gas. This can be used to power vehicles and generate electricity.

CHAPTER 7
DISEASE

Biologists are interested in everything about diseases – where they come from, how to treat them, and how they might change in the future.

Diseases are complex and affect people in different ways. Some are **infectious**, caused by bacteria or viruses that attack cells. They constantly evolve to resist any medicines designed to destroy them.

Some of the biggest killer diseases, including cancer and heart disease, are **non-infectious**. These diseases can be passed down in families through genes, or brought on by pollution, injury or even eating unhealthy food.

INFECTIOUS DISEASES

Some infectious diseases, such as malaria and flu, have been with humans for thousands of years. They're caused by things called **pathogens**. Here are some examples. Many of them are living microorganisms, but not all of them.

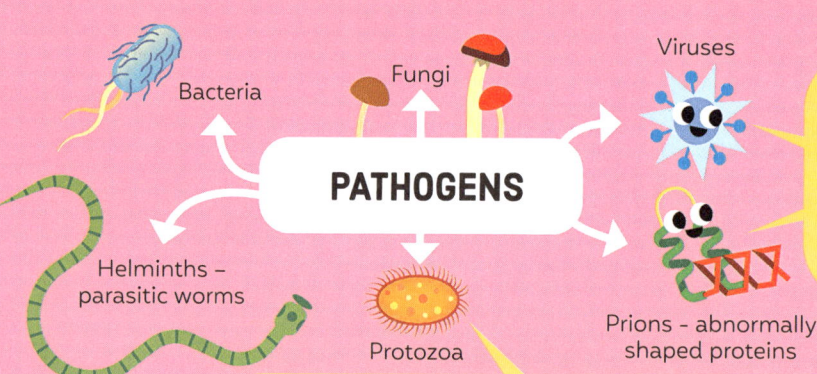

We're not considered to be alive because we don't meet all seven requirements for life (see page 8).

Some of us invade cells and multiply inside them before spreading to infect other cells.

CASE STUDY: LISTERIOSIS

This is caused by a bacterium called listeria and comes from infected food. Symptoms include fever, chills and stomach pain. Most people recover naturally from it. But, in rare cases, the bacteria travel through the blood to infect brain cells and tissue, causing a serious illness called meningitis. Here's how it works...

A listeria bacterium attaches to a cell in the lining of the gut.

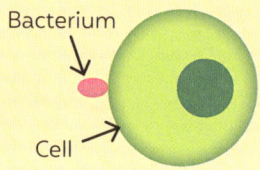

The cell's outer layer is tricked into wrapping around the bacterium.

The bacterium enters the cell.

It divides and multiplies inside the cell.

The bacteria grow tails and invade other cells.

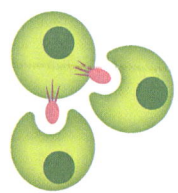

The body reacts to stop the infection. It's actually this reaction that causes fever and other symptoms.

VIRUSES

Viruses are much smaller than bacteria and come in all sorts of strange and remarkable shapes. They're made up of genetic material wrapped in a protein shell. To grow and reproduce, they must invade a living cell.

Spherical viruses, such as the coronavirus, have a spiky shell that helps them stick to and enter cells.

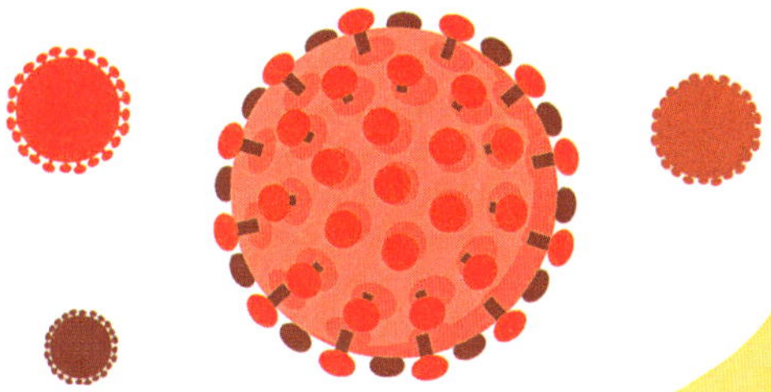

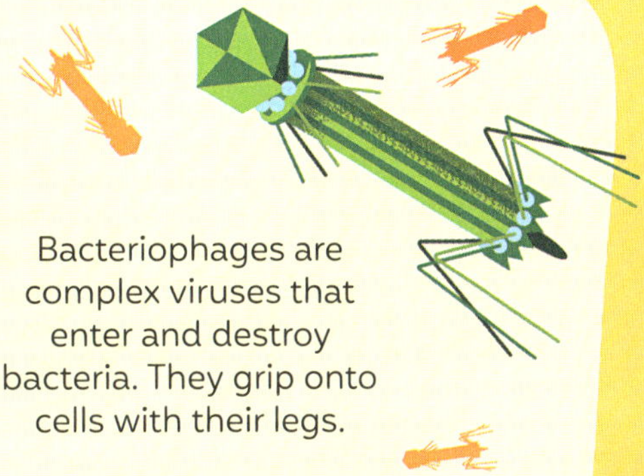

Bacteriophages are complex viruses that enter and destroy bacteria. They grip onto cells with their legs.

Once infected, a cell becomes a virus-making factory releasing copies of that virus to infect more cells.

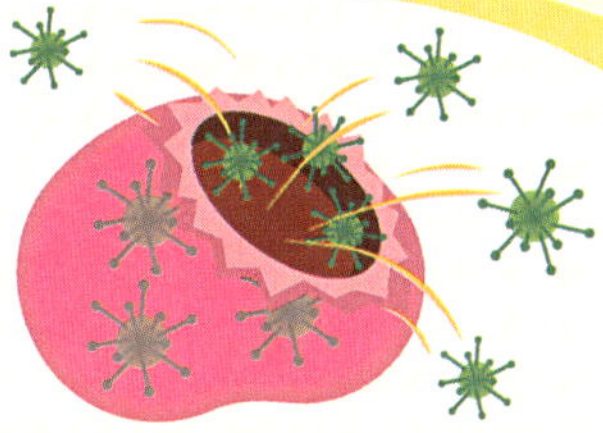

FIGHTING BACK

The human immune system is designed to expel invading pathogens. It uses **white blood cells** to attack them. Some white blood cells eat or engulf pathogens. Others make **antibodies** – proteins that attach to pathogens and destroy them or stick them together.

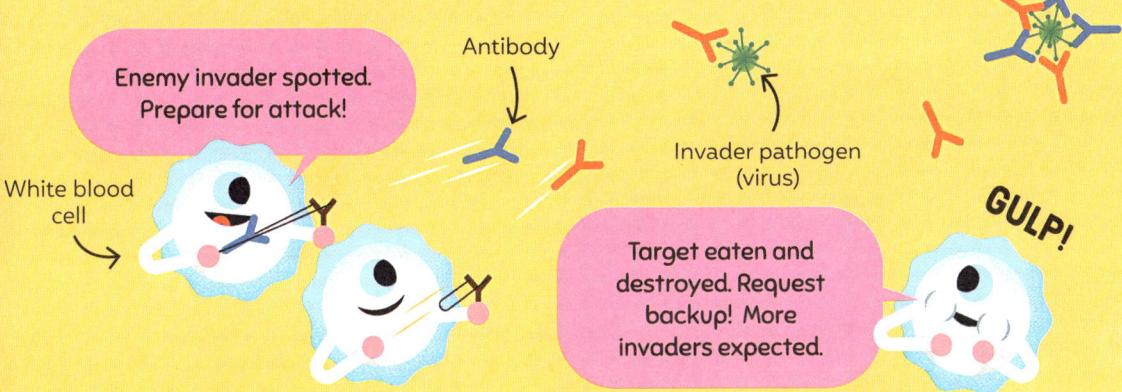

Antibody

Enemy invader spotted. Prepare for attack!

White blood cell

Invader pathogen (virus)

Target eaten and destroyed. Request backup! More invaders expected.

GULP!

People with strong immune systems are better able to fight disease – which is why some people in contact with pathogens don't get ill when others do.

WHAT ARE VACCINES?

For hundreds of years, people have known that if they catch certain diseases and survive, they rarely catch them again. They're said to be **immune**. Vaccines work a bit like this. They're a type of medicine that give you immunity against a particular disease.

"Many vaccines are made up of weak or dead versions of a pathogen."

"This injection contains a COVID-19 vaccine. After a few days, it triggers your immune system to create antibodies against covid."

"Now, you may get a slight temperature, but you won't get the full symptoms. And you won't get badly sick from covid!"

Vaccines for some diseases, such as polio or chickenpox, last a lifetime for most people. Vaccines for other diseases, such as tetanus, can weaken after ten years or so and require a booster dose.

"Why do some vaccines stop working after a time?"

"Pathogens evolve, just like plants and animals – some faster than others. So vaccines have to "evolve" too, to keep ahead."

"Is there a vaccine for a cold?"

"No. That's because a "cold" is the name for a group of symptoms caused by over 200 *different* viruses! So a vaccine against ONE cold virus will not protect you from others."

HOW VACCINES ARE MADE

Developing a new vaccine is a long, costly process that requires a huge amount of research and careful testing to make sure it's effective and safe. Here's how it's done.

RESEARCH AND DISCOVERY

Researchers focus on one pathogen and discover which type of vaccine works best against it.

PROOF

The vaccine is tested out lots and lots, first on small animals, then bigger ones. Finally – if it works – it's tested on people.

MAKING THE VACCINE

A manufacturer makes batches of the vaccine called **lots**. The lots are constantly tested to ensure they are safe to use.

VACCINE TESTING

Tests begin on small groups of people, then bigger groups. Researchers gather information on side effects and how well the vaccine works over time. This is known as a **clinical trial**.

APPROVAL

Data – from trials, the vaccine-making process and safety tests – is studied carefully. The vaccine is finally approved.

PUBLIC HEALTH CAMPAIGN

Government officials and doctors tell people about the vaccine, and encourage them to make appointments to have one.

CONSTANT MONITORING

The more people who get the vaccine, the harder it becomes for the disease to spread. Also, doctors get more information about how well the vaccine works. If there's a problem, it will be withdrawn.

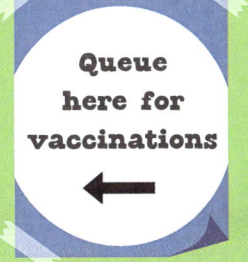

Queue here for vaccinations

HOW DISEASES SPREAD

Biologists and microbiologists try to pinpoint where diseases come from and how and why they spread. One theory is that many diseases began around 10,000 years ago. This was when people started farming and living closer to all sorts of animals.

Biologists today know that pathogens can and do jump from animals to humans, sometimes at a fast pace. Take yellow fever, for example...

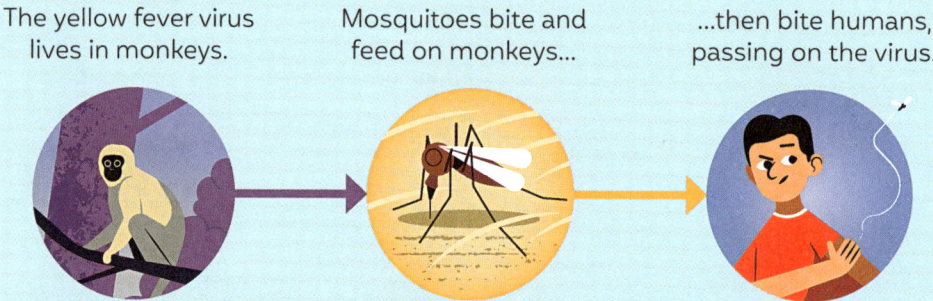

The yellow fever virus lives in monkeys.

Mosquitoes bite and feed on monkeys...

...then bite humans, passing on the virus.

Warmer, wetter weather is creating the perfect conditions for insects to breed and spread disease.

Lyme disease, spread by ticks, and malaria and dengue fever, spread by mosquitoes, are expanding into areas that are warmer due to climate change.

Tick

Mmm, human blood.

International travel doesn't help. It's easier than ever for a new virus to jump from one side of the world to another.

COUGH!

Bless you!

ACHOO!

HALTING THE SPREAD OF DISEASE

Better medicine and healthcare has reduced the number of deaths from disease in the last 50 years. But new treatments can also create new ways for diseases themselves to evolve or spread.

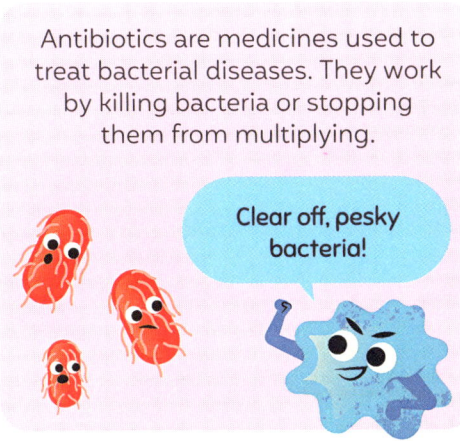

Antibiotics are medicines used to treat bacterial diseases. They work by killing bacteria or stopping them from multiplying.

Clear off, pesky bacteria!

But if antibiotics are used too often, bacteria build up a resistance to them so the antibiotics no longer work.

We've tried every antibiotic. None are working!

Some medical treatments for disease, such as blood transfusions and organ transplants, also create new ways to infect people.

Some surgeons have transplanted pigs' hearts into humans with severe heart disease, saving lives. But in one case, a pig virus was introduced to a patient and doctors were unable to treat it.

Only a handful of diseases can be eradicated permanently. We have to learn how to live with the rest.

Will we ever be able to stop diseases or will new ones keep on developing?

Does that mean making more and more medicines to prevent and treat diseases?

Yes, but many microbiologists think that the most effective way to fight disease is to strengthen the body's immune system. A lot of new research is being directed into this area.

FROM EPIDEMIC TO PANDEMIC

Outbreaks of diseases happen constantly, and they need to be stopped quickly before they spread. People who study the spread and control of diseases are known as **epidemiologists**.

What's the difference between an **epidemic** and a **pandemic**?

An epidemic is when a disease spreads quickly within a specific region. A pandemic is when a disease spreads quickly between countries – and around the world.

The coronavirus (COVID-19) pandemic in 2019 resulted in the deaths of 27 million people. Will there be another pandemic?

Most experts think it's likely to happen one day, but no one can predict when. It might be decades before the next one.

Many factors enable new pathogens to emerge and spread, and known pathogens to re-emerge.

Is it possible to prevent a pandemic?

Countries can keep up their vaccine stocks and make plans to control early disease outbreaks. They are hoping to develop new vaccines that might help prevent new pathogens, too.

Epidemiologists use maps to plot disease outbreaks. That means they can track where a disease is most infectious and tell people to stay away.

COVID-19 TEST SITE

CASE HISTORY: THE 1918 FLU PANDEMIC

The 1918 flu, also known as the Spanish flu, was a devastating virus that spread around the world from 1918-1920. In many cases, the disease developed into severe pneumonia, leaving patients struggling for breath.

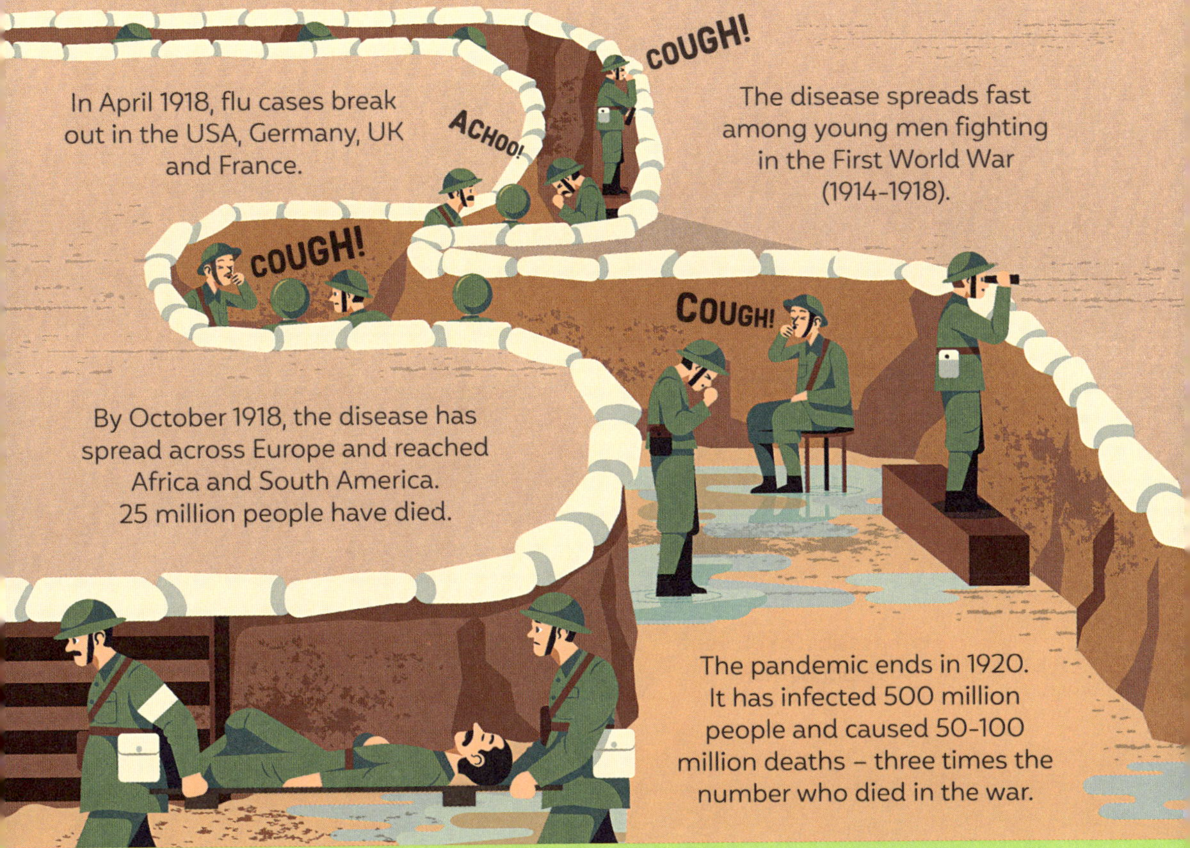

In April 1918, flu cases break out in the USA, Germany, UK and France.

The disease spreads fast among young men fighting in the First World War (1914-1918).

By October 1918, the disease has spread across Europe and reached Africa and South America. 25 million people have died.

The pandemic ends in 1920. It has infected 500 million people and caused 50-100 million deaths – three times the number who died in the war.

Biologists today still investigate diseases from the past to discover what made them so deadly. In the 1990s, scientists recovered a preserved sample of the 1918 flu virus from a body buried under ice in Alaska, USA. In 2005, they identified the virus's full genome sequence.

We are investigating the exact genes and mutations that caused the 1918 flu virus. This will help us spot severe forms of flu in the future and design drugs in time to stop another pandemic.

Hmm. Is it safe to work on deadly viruses? Someone could, by accident or just maybe on purpose, leak that 1918 virus and CAUSE another pandemic...

NON-INFECTIOUS DISEASES

Non-infectious diseases may not *sound* scary, because you can't catch them from other people. But most deaths in the world are caused by them – around 40 million a year.

What's the difference between infectious and non-infectious diseases?

Non-infectious diseases are not caused by pathogens. They may develop from genes or from lifestyle choices, such as smoking. They also develop slowly and can last a long time.

Which non-infectious diseases cause the most harm?

Heart disease, cancer, diabetes and chronic lung disease result in the most deaths. But many people with these diseases are able to live long lives.

Can these diseases be prevented?

Some can be prevented by avoiding **risk factors** – things that increase the likelihood of getting a disease.

What are some of the main risk factors?

Not exercising, eating too much fatty food or breathing in polluted air. Some risk factors you can control, but not all.

RISK FACTORS SUCH AS...

An unhealthy diet	Stress	Injury	Pollution
Too little exercise	Too much alcohol	Too much sugar	Too much salt
Obesity	Smoking	Radiation	Gene disorders

...CAN LEAD TO SOME OF THESE DISEASES

- Cancer
- Diabetes
- Lung disease
- Heart disease and stroke
- Asthma

When researching new treatments, scientists investigate how to identify a disease, how it spreads and what triggers it. There are many different treatments, from medicine that kills cells to surgically removing organs.

HEART DISEASE

This is the biggest killer of adults over 40. It includes conditions such as **atherosclerosis** – a build-up of fatty substances in the arteries.

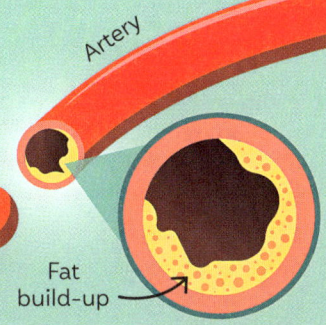

Artery

Fat build-up

Blocked arteries reduce the flow of oxygen-rich blood to the body. This can cause a heart attack or a stroke.

Scientists are investigating all kinds of heart cells and molecules to see how they interact. They've identified some heart-damaging molecules, and are developing medicines to block them.

CANCER

Cancer is a group of diseases that cause cells to grow uncontrollably.

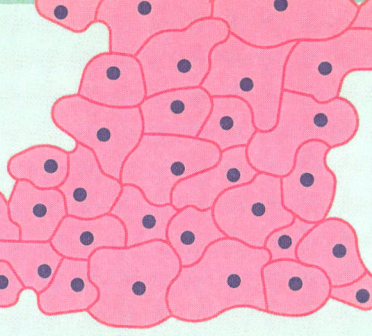

If cancer cells are not removed and continue to grow, they can spread to other parts of the body. This can make people very sick – but there are treatments.

Scientists are researching new forms of medication, including cancer vaccines. They're also identifying the genes, molecules and DNA changes that cause cancer in individual patients. This will help them design tailor-made treatment plans.

HUNTINGTON'S DISEASE

This can develop from a gene disorder, or mutation, passed from one or both parents. It causes brain cells to break down and die. There is still no cure, but in 1993, scientists discovered the gene that causes it.

Normal brain section

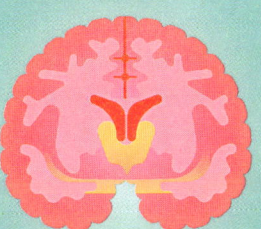

Brain with Huntington's

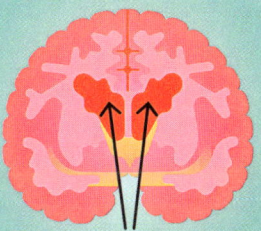

Dead areas of the brain

Genetic engineers have developed new techniques that involve inserting genetic material into cells to slow down the disease.

105

CHAPTER 8
BIG QUESTIONS

There are all sorts of mysteries about living things that biologists are yet to solve, from the possibility of life in space to whether we could live forever. We may never know the answers for sure.

What is cloning and how can we use it? Can your environment change your genes? What amazing abilities do animals have – and can we copy them?

These are just some of the exciting areas of research that biologists are investigating right now.

LIFE IN THE UNIVERSE

Is there life on another planet? **Astrobiologists** are hoping to find places that have the right conditions to support life in the universe. One place that *might* satisfy these conditions is Mars.

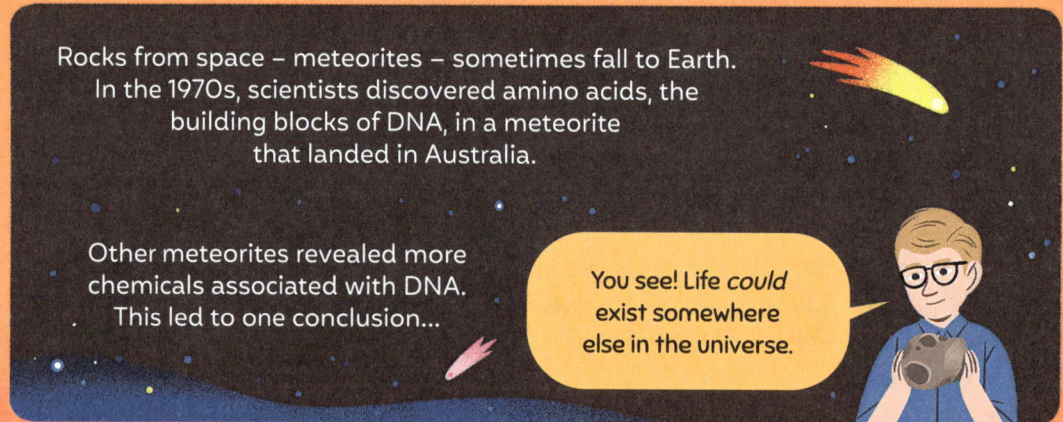

Rocks from space – meteorites – sometimes fall to Earth. In the 1970s, scientists discovered amino acids, the building blocks of DNA, in a meteorite that landed in Australia.

Other meteorites revealed more chemicals associated with DNA. This led to one conclusion...

You see! Life *could* exist somewhere else in the universe.

The search for life in space often starts with the search for water and food – both essential to support life. When rocks from Mars revealed it once contained rivers, lakes and seas, scientists began to investigate further.

In 2021, NASA dropped a robot rover on Mars called *Perseverance*.

It travels about looking for evidence of water and gathering soil and rock samples to take back to Earth.

Perseverance is also looking for evidence of **extremophiles** – organisms, such as archaea, that can survive in extreme locations.

TOUGH TARDIGRADES

Meet the **tardigrade**, also known as a moss piglet – one of Earth's toughest extremophiles. It lives in mild habitats, but can cope in VERY tough ones, too.

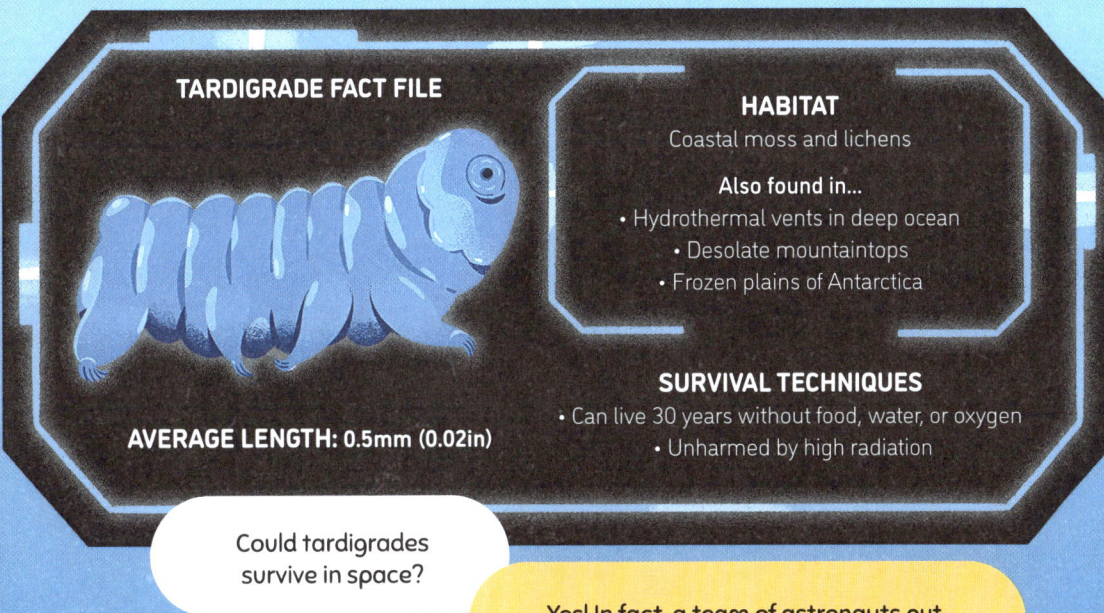

TARDIGRADE FACT FILE

AVERAGE LENGTH: 0.5mm (0.02in)

HABITAT
Coastal moss and lichens

Also found in...
- Hydrothermal vents in deep ocean
- Desolate mountaintops
- Frozen plains of Antarctica

SURVIVAL TECHNIQUES
- Can live 30 years without food, water, or oxygen
- Unharmed by high radiation

> Could tardigrades survive in space?

> Yes! In fact, a team of astronauts put a box of tardigrades in outer space for a month. Most came home unharmed and continued to reproduce as normal.

> That's amazing! How do they do it?

> Part of their secret is in their genes. Some are activated by radiation to provide protection. Tiny cell sensors also trigger a state of deep hibernation that helps them survive.

> Neat!

> Wait til you hear THIS. We tried combining tardigrade DNA with human cells. Those cells were better at surviving exposure to radiation than normal human cells.

> Cool!

> Right! Studying extremophiles also gives us an idea of the kind of chemicals to look for when searching for life on other planets or moons.

COULD WE LIVE FOREVER?

Some organisms live much longer than humans. Biologists are sure there are ways to help extend our lifespans, and even reverse the ageing process. But, living *forever*? Read on...

Why do some things live longer than others?

We think that an organism's maximum lifespan is programmed into its genes. Humans typically live for 70–100 years, depending on our environment and lifestyle. But the tortoise you're sitting on is 150 years old, and counting.

There's even an organism that may be programmed not to die at all. Take a look at the incredible life cycle of the immortal jellyfish.

The immortal jellyfish begins its life as a tiny larva.

It develops into something called a polyp...

...which produces several adult jellyfish.

When each jellyfish gets old or injured, it turns *back* into a polyp. This can happen again and again – maybe forever – we don't know.

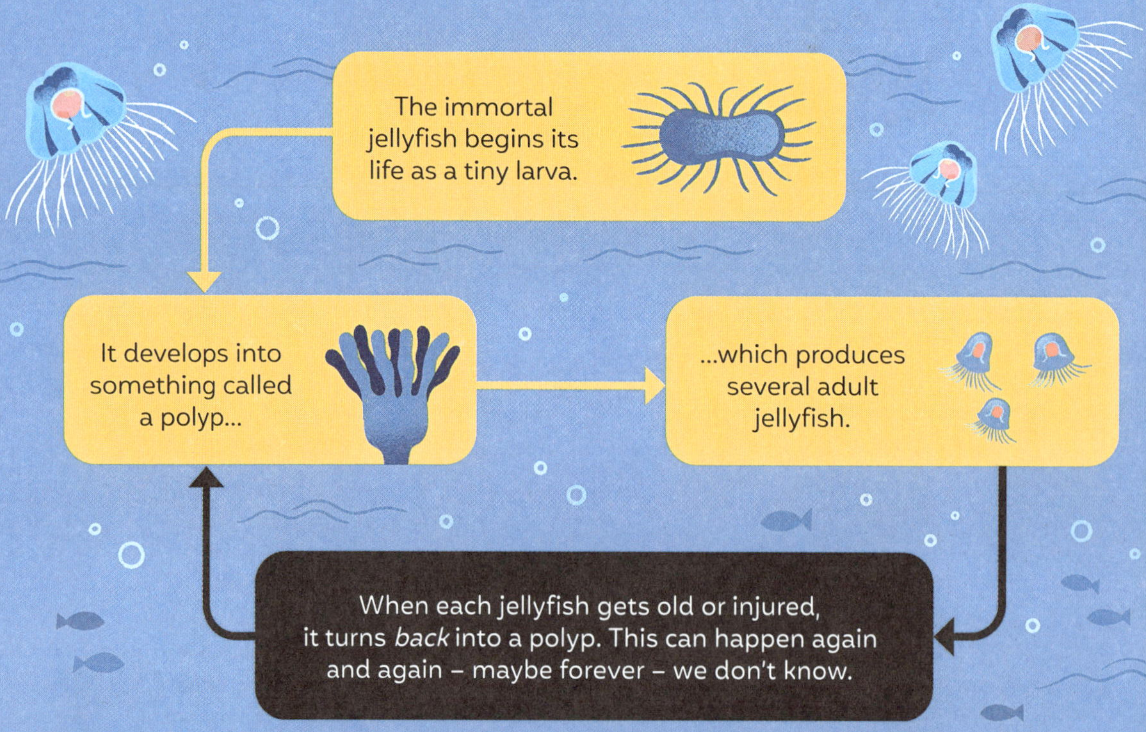

Immortal jellyfish can still die if they're eaten or catch a disease. But, in theory, they can't die of old age. This is known as **biological immortality**.

A big cause of ageing in humans, and many other species, lies in our cells. As we get older, more of our cells get damaged and become **senescent**. This means the cells don't die, but they can't repair themselves either. They're nicknamed **zombie cells**.

As zombie cells build up in our bodies, they damage our organs. But biologists are researching ways to defeat them.

One way is to develop new drugs that help our bodies kill zombie cells and clear them out.

Another way is to genetically edit zombie cells so they revert back to a younger, healthier state.

So if you manage to eliminate zombie cells, does that mean you *could* live forever?

I don't think so, no. It could increase our lifespan by several years though, maybe even decades.

Ah well. Maybe immortality wouldn't be such a good idea anyway...

I agree. Many biologists are far more interested in improving our *healthspan* – the amount of time we stay healthy. Targeting zombie cells can help with that too.

WHAT MAKES YOU *YOU*?

Your genes have a huge effect on what your body looks like. But they also affect your personality. The question is, how much? Is personality more to do with your genes, or the environment you grow up in? It's a question people have been debating for decades.

THINGS THAT DETERMINE WHO YOU ARE

Genes · Money · School · Community and culture · Health · Nutrition · TV · Social media · Early childhood experiences · Family or carers · Books · Teachers

Seems as if genes are only a small factor?

In fact, genes might be the BIGGEST factor, even on your mood. Some studies have found that how happy a person is, can be around 50% to do with their genes.

How on Earth did they test THAT?!

They sent in-depth questionnaires to thousands of identical twins. They share identical DNA but have had different life experiences. This helped researchers calculate how much their happiness depended on their genes.

There's lots of research that shows how genes determine personality traits, such as the ability to solve problems or react under stress. But recent studies also suggest that *experiences* can actually *change your genes*.

DO EXPERIENCES CHANGE YOU?

Stress is a part of everyday life. You may feel stressed about meeting someone for the first time or moving home, for example. But it turns out that *extreme* stress may change the way your genes behave. **Epigenetics** is a new area of biology that looks into this.

Here's a study carried out by epigeneticists about how extreme stress, or **trauma**, affects genes.

During the winter of 1944-1945, in the Second World War, parts of the Netherlands suffered from a severe famine.

Pregnant women gave birth to babies who were altered by the famine their whole lives.

Many developed health problems as adults, such as heart disease and depression.

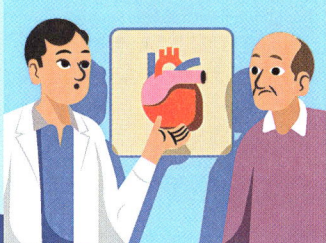

Epigeneticists examined the DNA of these adults.

They discovered a chemical that had attached to some of their genes. The chemical STOPPED the genes from switching on, which affected their long-term health. And the genes have been switched off ever since.

So stress can affect the long-term health of an unborn child?!

Well, that's the theory. And the genetic changes can be passed on to the next generation too. The physical and mental health of a pregnant woman could affect her children AND future grandchildren.

It seems that genes and the environment BOTH determine who you are. But which is more significant remains a mystery and is continuing to keep scientists busy.

WHAT IS CLONING?

Cloning means making a genetically identical copy of an organism. It happens in nature, but biologists are also able to clone organisms artificially.

Many organisms clone themselves as a way to reproduce.

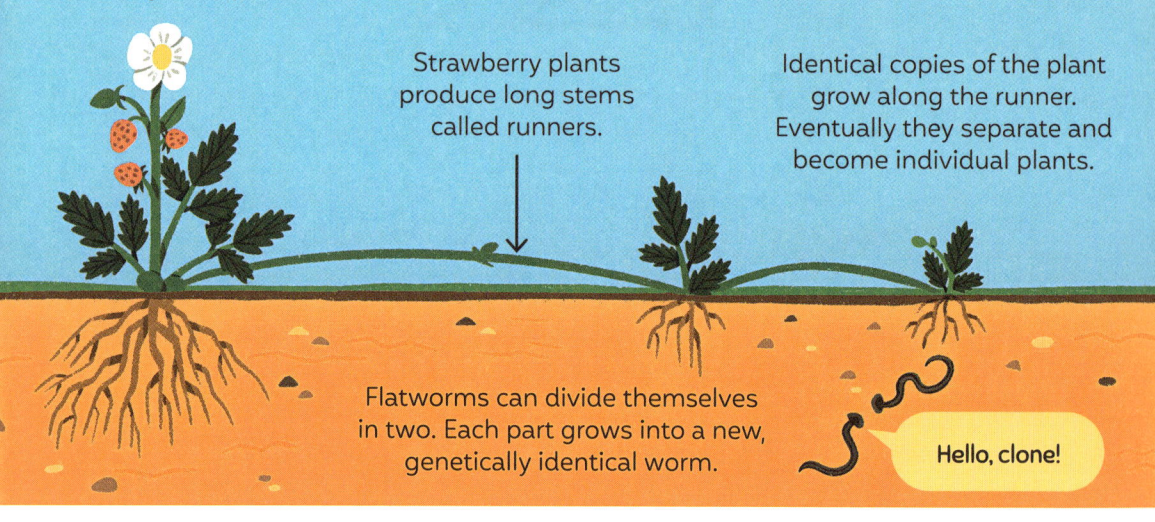

Strawberry plants produce long stems called runners.

Identical copies of the plant grow along the runner. Eventually they separate and become individual plants.

Flatworms can divide themselves in two. Each part grows into a new, genetically identical worm.

Hello, clone!

In 1996, biologists created the first mammal clone – a sheep called Dolly. Here's how they did it.

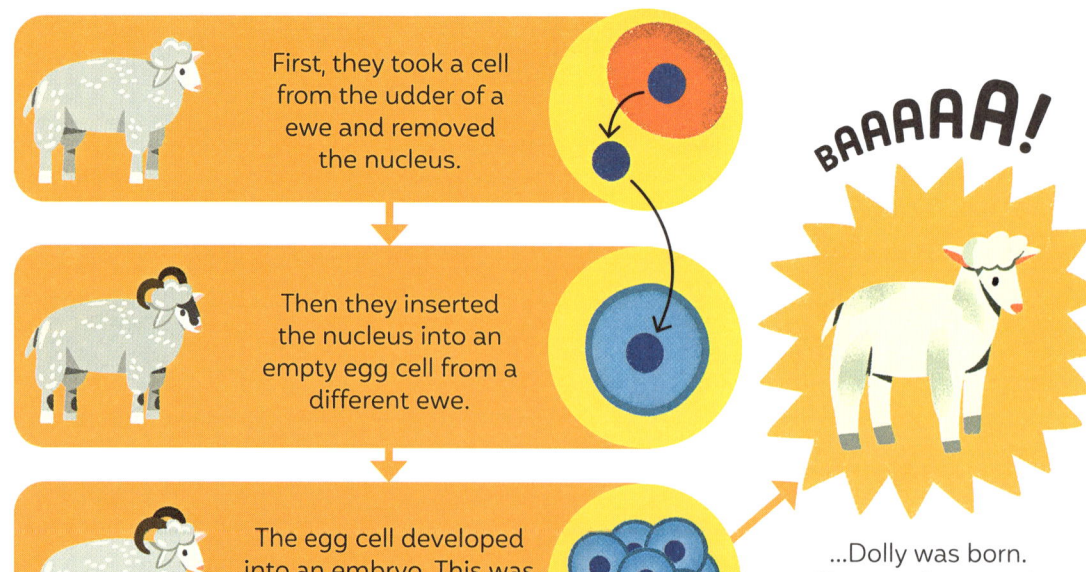

First, they took a cell from the udder of a ewe and removed the nucleus.

Then they inserted the nucleus into an empty egg cell from a different ewe.

The egg cell developed into an embryo. This was implanted inside a third ewe where it grew, until...

BAAAAA!

...Dolly was born. She was the genetic clone of the first sheep – but six years younger.

Cloning is a complicated process and it doesn't always work. But it has all sorts of potential uses.

Crops with desirable traits, including disease-resistance, are cloned to help boost food production.

Endangered animals, such as the black-footed ferret, have been cloned to help save them from extinction.

Biologists are also researching ways to clone human cells, such as skin cells or heart cells, to help repair damaged organs.

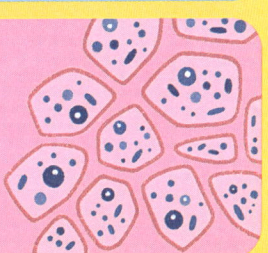

Can you make a clone of a person that's an exact copy of how they are NOW?

No, that's complete science fiction. But we *could* clone a human using the same method as we used to create Dolly the sheep. It would be highly controversial though. In most countries it's illegal.

Animal clones often develop health problems that cut short their lives. We don't know what the long-term effects might be in humans.

It raises other questions too. Would a clone be considered the child of the original human, or their identical twin – or a copy?

Would clones have the same rights as other people?

115

1,000 YEARS AFTER HUMANS

Forests expand to cover much of the land. This helps reduce CO_2 levels.

By now, most buildings are gone – only stone structures and plastic waste remain.

Biodiversity surges. Species either adapt or die out.

Ocean habitats such as coral reefs gradually recover from pollution and high temperatures.

1,000,000 YEARS AFTER HUMANS

The climate continues to go through natural cycles of warming and cooling. Eventually, Earth enters another ice age – but it won't last forever.

New species evolve as the planet changes. Perhaps a new type of intelligent life emerges to fill the gap left by humans.

Oh no, not again...

The only signs that humans ever existed are under the ground.

AMAZING ANIMAL SENSES

It turns out that animals have all sorts of remarkable senses that humans don't. Here are four examples.

TRACKING UNDERWATER

Seals can detect underwater trails left by shoals of fish up to 100m (330ft) away. Their sensitive whiskers can pick up evidence of slightly disturbed water long after the fish have passed.

HEAT SENSING

Vampire bats survive by drinking the blood of mammals and birds. To do this, they have nerve endings around their noses that sense heat, in the form of infrared radiation, from blood. This allows them to detect blood-filled veins, so they know exactly where to bite.

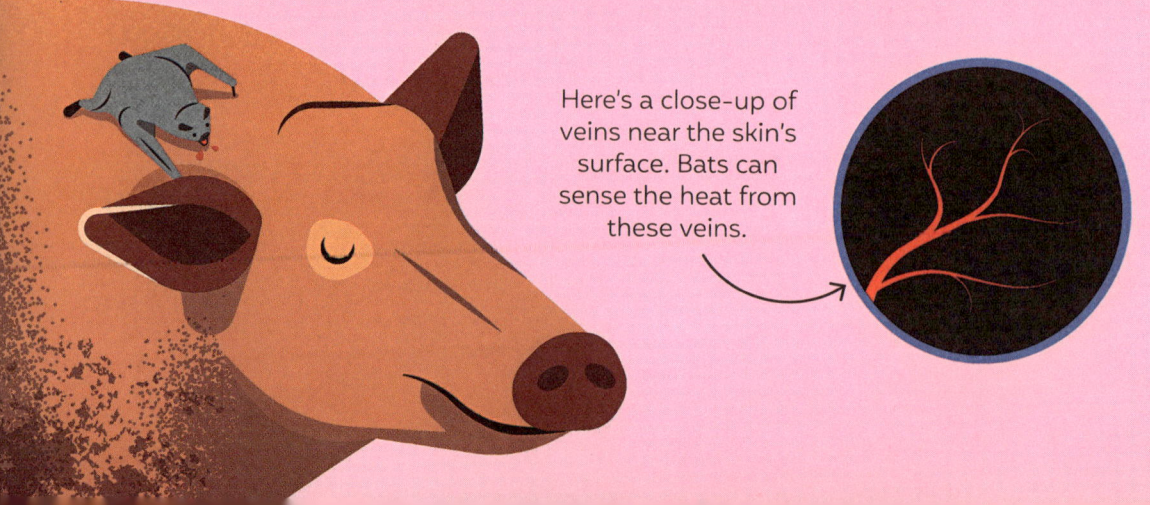

MAGNETIC FIELDS

The Earth has a magnetic field which makes compasses point north. Birds, snakes, turtles and some other animals can sense this field. They use it to find their way and migrate huge distances across the world.

Biologists have discovered magnetic chemicals in the eyes of migratory birds, such as European robins.

The chemicals work like an internal compass to help robins follow directions, so they don't get lost.

ELECTROMAGNETIC FIELDS

Bees have a sense that detects a really subtle thing: electromagnetism. It helps them find flowers with nectar for them to eat. It works because things in nature often have either a positive or negative electromagnetic charge, and because opposite charges attract.

So, bees and flowers are attracted to each other?

Yes. Flowers typically have a negative charge. And bees in flight have a positive charge, which helps them find flowers.

And there's more! The same sense tells if a rival bee has just been feeding on a flower. So, bees know which flowers to avoid.

NATURE-INSPIRED TECHNOLOGY

Some of the most amazing technology humans have invented has been inspired by living organisms. This is known as **biomimicry**. Here are some examples.

The way drones hover and change direction was inspired by hummingbirds.

Many fish have a super-wide range of vision – nearly 360 degrees. A type of wide-angle camera lens, called a fish-eye lens, is based on this design.

These wind turbine blades have bumps like humpback whale flippers. This shape helps them move through the air more efficiently.

Spider silk is incredibly strong yet lightweight. It has inspired the creation of super-strong fabrics that can be used to make ropes and bulletproof vests.

Geckos have tiny hairs on their feet that help them grip walls. Scientists have copied this to create a glue-free sticking method that can be used in bandages and climbing robots.

Scientists are developing microscopic robots called nanorobots. They're designed to move like bacteria through your blood vessels.

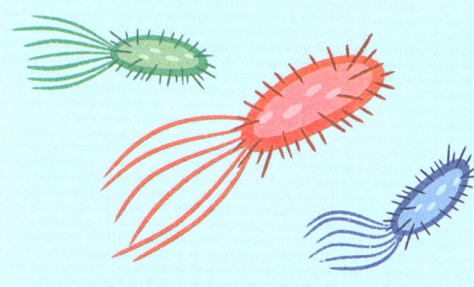

Once inside, they can monitor your health and send information back to a computer. They can also deliver medicines directly to specific body parts.

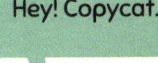

There's even a pangolin-style backpack! The overlapping scales make it tough yet flexible.

Hey! Copycat.

BIOLOGY ALL AROUND

You don't have to be in a lab to do biology. You can do it anywhere. Here are a few ideas for exploring biology wherever you are.

TREE WATCHING

Pick a tree or plant you can observe easily through the year. It could be in a park or garden or a street near your home. Watch how it changes in different months. You could take photos, make sketches or keep a diary.

ANIMAL SPOTTING

When you're in a garden or going for a walk, keep an eye out for nature all around you. Look under stones for **invertebrates** – animals lacking a backbone, such as insects. Look up to see birds. Stop to watch what they do.

Ooh, look how they move to avoid the light.

I wonder why they're gathering in a line...

ASKING QUESTIONS

Find out more about the plants and creatures you have seen by going to a library, reading books or looking online.

LIFE IS EVERYWHERE

Everywhere they look, biologists are always finding NEW species. From the tiniest cells to vast ecosystems, no matter how remote and how far apart their environments are, ALL organisms are connected in an ever-changing, endless parade of LIFE.

We're all connected!

JOBS IN BIOLOGY

Biology is useful for a HUGE range of jobs. Some are done in labs. Others involve exploring rainforests or oceans – or even other planets. Here are just a few of them.

Astrobiologists study the possibility of life in the universe, beyond Earth.

Bioarchaeologists look at the biological remains of past human civilizations, such as bones and DNA.

Biochemists investigate genes, cells and the chemical reactions and processes of life.

Bioinformatics scientists use computer techniques to study evolutionary changes and biological data, such as genetic sequences.

Botanists study everything to do with plants.

Conservationists help protect living things and their habitats. They work on projects to save biodiversity.

Epidemiologists try to stop or prevent diseases. They study the cause and location of outbreaks.

Forensic scientists study scientific evidence from crime scenes to help with police investigations.

Genetic engineers manipulate genes and transfer them between species to create new or improved organisms.

Marine biologists study sea organisms and habitats, such as coral reefs.

Microbiologists investigate and find cures for diseases caused by viruses and other pathogens.

Park rangers educate people about animals, plants and habitats. They also monitor and protect wildlife.

Pathologists do tests on bodies, including dead bodies, to diagnose diseases or find the cause of death.

Physiotherapists help patients get their body moving and working well, often after injury, surgery or an illness.

Soil scientists study the quality of soil, and suggest ways to improve it, often for farming or conservation.

Zoologists study animals in the wild and in zoos. Many zoologists are involved in projects to save animals from extinction.

GLOSSARY

This glossary explains some of the words used in this book. Words in *italics* are explained in other entries.

amino acid a kind of building-block chemical that makes up *proteins*.

bacterium (plural: bacteria) a kind of *microorganism*, usually made of just one *cell*, that often lives inside another *organism*.

biodiversity the range of different *species* in the world or in a particular area.

carbon dioxide a gas in the air. Plants use it during *photosynthesis* to make sugars.

cells the basic building blocks of all living things – some are made of a single cell.

cloning the ability of some creatures to make copies of themselves.

decomposition the process of breaking down dead *organisms*, so that they become nutrients for other life forms.

DNA a complex chemical found in most *cells* that holds the instructions for a living thing to grow and survive.

ecology the study of how *organisms* interact with their *habitat*.

embryo a small collection of *cells* that is one of the earliest stages of life for most multi-celled *organisms*.

environment the surroundings of an *organism*, including other living things and non-living things.

evolution the way that living things very gradually change over many generations, usually so that they are better adapted for their *environment*.

extinction the dying out of a *species*.

extremophiles *species* able to live and thrive in extreme *environments*.

fossils the remains of long-dead *organisms*, that are preserved as stone.

genes sections of *DNA* that give individual *cells* specific instructions. For example, some genes control how tall a person is.

habitat the *environment* in which a *species* naturally lives.

mass extinction event the loss of over 75% of Earth's *species* within hundreds of thousands of years – a relatively short period of time compared to *evolution*.

microorganism a tiny living thing, such as a *bacterium*, only visible through a microscope.

organelle part of a *cell* that carries out a particular job.

organism a living thing.

parasite an *organism* that lives on or in another organism and gets food from it.

pathogen an *organism* or infectious agent such as a *virus*, that causes disease.

photosynthesis the process plants use to convert sunlight into food.

protein an essential chemical used by *organisms* for growth, repair and making structures, such as muscles or bones.

species a group of *organisms* that look alike and can reproduce together.

stem cell a *cell* before it has specialized to carry out a particular role in an *organism*.

taxonomy a grouping system that helps biologists identify and classify *organisms*.

traits features that make an *organism* distinct from another and that can be passed on to offspring.

virus a microscopically small thing that is not itself alive, but can infect and reproduce inside the *cells* of living things.

INDEX

adapting, 47-57, 117
ageing, 110-111
algae, 6, 13, 24, 74, 75
amino acids, 18, 19, 29, 108
anatomy, 60-63, 64
animals, 6, 12, 14, 24, 25, 100, 118-119
   cells, 28, 29, 36, 38, 40, 84, 114
   evolution, 48-57
antibiotics, 13, 35, 43, 93, 101
antibodies, 97, 98
archaea, 13, 33, 35, 108
Arctic, the, 79, 85
asteroids, 19, 23, 25, 108
astrobiology, 7, 108-109

bacteria, 13, 20-21, 28, 31, 32, 35, 42, 43, 66-67, 88, 92, 93, 96, 97, 101, 121
biodiversity, 43, 82, 85, 117
biofuels, 93
blood, 31, 45, 62, 63, 96, 105, 118, 121
bones, 32, 52, 60, 62
brain, 36, 60, 62, 64-65, 67, 105

cancer, 104, 105
cane toads, 76-77
carbon dioxide, 72, 78, 81, 117
cells, 5, 7, 8, 22, 24, 27-45, 62, 68, 84, 96, 105, 111, 114
   brain, 36, 64, 96, 105
   red blood, 28, 31, 32, 35, 36, 44
   sex, 38, 63, 84
   stem, 39, 40, 41
   white blood, 36, 63, 66, 97
   zombie, 111
Chernobyl, 89
classification, see taxonomy
climate change, 24, 25, 54-55, 72-75, 100, 117
cloning, 9, 114-115
co-evolution, 56-57
common ancestor, 17, 22, 23, 52
conservation, 73-81, 84-85
coral, 74-75, 117
COVID-19, 98, 102
cyanobacteria, 20-21, 24

Darwin, Charles, 50-53
decomposers, 88-89, 91
deforestation, 82, 83
digestive system, 32, 63, 66-67
dinosaurs, 25, 52
diseases, 7, 35, 41, 60, 95-105
   infectious, 96-103
   non-infectious, 104-105
   resistance, 43, 115
dissection, 60
DNA, 22, 29, 35, 38, 42, 44-45, 48, 68-69, 78, 108
   sequencing, 69
drought, 43, 82

ecology, 7, 71-85
electromagnetic fields, 119
embryos, 38, 41, 73, 84, 114
environment, 33, 43, 52, 53, 54, 71, 76, 83, 112, 113, 116-117
enzymes, 88
epigenetics, 113
eukaryotes, 24, 35
evolution, 6, 23, 24-25, 47-57, 77, 98, 117
extinction, 24, 25, 55, 72, 84, 85, 115
extremophiles, 33, 108, 109

fermentation, 92-93
forensic science, 44, 45
First World War, 103
fossils, 21, 24, 52
frozen zoos, 84
fungi, 9, 13, 24, 32, 83, 88, 90-91, 92, 96

Galápagos Islands, 50, 51
genes, 29, 39, 42-43, 68-69, 77, 104, 105, 109, 110, 112-113
genetic engineering, 42-43, 109, 111, 114
global warming, 55, 72-75, 78, 79, 81
green deserts, 83

habitats, 55, 72-83, 116, 117
healthspan, 111
Hooke, Robert, 30, 31
human body, 6, 28, 29, 32, 36, 59-69, 97, 101, 104-105, 111

Human Genome Project, 69
Humongous Fungus, 91
hydrothermal vents, 19, 33, 109

ice ages, 23, 117
immortality, 110-111
immune system, 63, 97, 98, 101,
insulin, 42, 93

kingdoms, 12-13, 14

life, definition of, 8-9, 62-63, 96
lifespan, 110, 111
Linnaeus, Carl, 16
LUCA (Last Universal Common Ancestor), 22-23, 24

magnetic fields, 60, 119
Mars, 108
mass extinction, 24, 25, 72, 85
medicines, 7, 41, 87, 93, 98-99, 101, 105, 121
mental health, 67, 113
meteors, see asteroids
microorganisms, 13, 19, 20, 24, 28, 31, 32, 33, 42, 66-67, 87-93, 96, 121
microscopes, 5, 30-31
migration, 4, 54, 79, 119
mimicry, 57, 120-121
   animals, 57
   technology, 120-121
mitosis, 37
MRI (Magnetic Resonance Imaging), 60, 61
mutualism, 57, 74, 80, 90
mycorrhizal networks, 90

natural selection, 48-49, 51, 52, 53, 54-55
neuroplasticity, 65
nutrients, 8, 63, 66, 74, 80, 83, 88, 90, 91

organelles, 29, 34
origins of life, 18-24, 53

palm oil, 83
pandemics, 102, 103
parasites, 91, 96
pathogens, 96-97, 98, 100, 102
peat, 78

photosynthesis, 8, 81, 90
physiology, 62-63
plants, 6, 8, 9, 12, 24, 30, 34, 38, 43, 80, 83, 85, 88, 90, 114, 116, 122
   cells, 29, 30-31, 34
   crops, 43, 83, 85, 93, 115
pollution, 91, 104, 116
populations, 49, 76, 77, 78, 116
primordial soup, 18
proteins, 29, 92, 96, 97
public health campaigns, 99

radiation, 21, 89, 104, 109, 118
radiometric dating, 21
rainforests, 80-81, 82
reproduction, 9, 23, 38, 48, 63, 73, 84, 97, 114
robots, 108, 121

Second World War, 113
seed banks, 85
simulations, 19, 61
soil, 78, 83, 88, 89
space, 7, 19, 85, 108-109
species, 15, 16, 17, 24, 25, 48, 49, 50, 54, 55, 56, 57, 68, 74, 80, 81
   endangered, 77, 82, 84, 115, 116
   new, 51, 117, 123
   saving, 72, 74, 75, 77, 78, 79, 84, 85

tardigrades, 109
targeted gene flow, 77
taxonomy, 12-17
tracking animals, 73-82, 118
traits, 29, 42, 43, 48-52, 54, 68-69, 112, 115
trauma, 113
trees, 12, 35, 57, 80-83, 89, 90, 122

vaccines, 93, 98-99, 102, 105
van Leeuwenhoek, Antonie, 31
viruses, 32, 43, 96-103
Vesalius, Andreas, 60

wildfires, 72, 82

yeast, 13, 28, 91

ACKNOWLEDGEMENTS

Written by Lizzie Cope & Minna Lacey

Illustrated by Anton Hallmann & Hannah Li

Edited by Alex Frith

Designed by Samuel Gorham

Biology expert: Dr. Colin Dodd

Series editor: Jane Chisholm

Series designer: Freya Harrison

First published in 2025 by Usborne Publishing Limited, 83-85 Saffron Hill, London EC1N 8RT, United Kingdom. usborne.com

Copyright © 2025 Usborne Publishing Limited. The name Usborne and the Balloon logo are registered trade marks of Usborne Publishing Limited. All rights reserved. No part of this publication may be reproduced or used in any manner for the purpose of training artificial intelligence technologies or systems (including for text or data mining), stored in retrieval systems or transmitted in any form or by any means without prior permission of the publisher. UKE